The
SAVVY SHOPPER'S
Cookbook

To Paul, for believing in every mad idea I've ever had.

With love, A x

The
SAVVY SHOPPER'S
Cookbook

AMY SHEPPARD

EBURY
PRESS

CONTENTS

INTRODUCTION

Like everybody else, I had heard about the meteoric rise of discount supermarkets. Friends had tried for ages to convince me of the savings and quality that they were offering; but I didn't want to change – I hate change! When I finally ventured into my local discount supermarket, I felt like I was walking into a party I hadn't been invited to. There was an aura of contented smugness to the customers, wandering around as though part of a special secret club. It was confusing at first, but I did what I'd come to do. I shopped. I shopped and I saved – massively. And then I understood the smugness...

These shops are not the size of aircraft hangars, which require an hour of careful navigation to fill even the smallest of trolleys. They do not sell 18 different types of tomato ketchup (that's right, I counted). You do not have to wade through overcomplicated special offers or have discounted food dangled in front of your trolley. They are simple, direct, and they do what they say on the tins(!). I was fully converted, and have never looked back.

However, there can be a few drawbacks. When I first made the switch, I continued to get at least one bag of shopping from another, more traditional, supermarket each week. I was making the same meals I always had, and I simply couldn't get all of the ingredients I needed. What's more, neither could my friends. Then, it occurred to me that it was the recipes that I needed to change, not the supermarket. So I went back to the drawing board.

I realised that these discount supermarkets are a cook's heaven. They are ingredient-led and, as a result, ingredient rich. I was even able to come up with recipes using ingredients that I would never have dreamt of using in a midweek meal before, because of the high cost of them when purchased elsewhere.

So there it is: my concept for a cookery book. Soups and Snacks, Sides and Salads, Fish, Vegetarian, Chicken, Beef and Pork and Sweet Treats, all made using simple, discount supermarket ingredients, all of which can be bought from the leading discount supermarkets.

To get the best out of a discount super-market, you need to think like a discount supermarket!... These recipes aren't just about budget cooking; they are about scaling down your food shop and making more from less. You won't find complicated methods or long ingredient lists. It's about simplifying your shopping and your cooking. That's where the real savings lie, both in time and money.

If you're looking for a cookbook to make impressive dinner party food, this one might not be for you! If, however, you're looking for simple but delicious, cheap and, for the most part, healthy midweek dinner or lunch ideas to match your shopping habits, this might be just what you've been searching for.

a note on the RECIPES

I have tried to make the recipes in this book as simple as possible, both in execution and explanation. I am assuming that, as you have bought this book, clearly you have an interest in food, so I don't need to explain in exhaustive detail how to chop an onion. You know how to chop an onion!

I don't include total cooking or preparation time in any of my recipes. This is for two reasons. Firstly, I find that few people ever look at cooking times in recipe books. Secondly, you don't know how long it takes me to chop a carrot, or grate some cheese, and I don't know how long it takes you! I will, of course, tell you how long something needs to be in the oven, on the hob or in the microwave, but the prep time is up to you as you juggle everything else you might be doing that day.

You won't see long lists of ingredients in this book either. I love simplicity in cooking. All of the ingredients I use bring something to the table or they don't go in the dish. You can be sure that if the recipe calls for it, it needs to be included.

Having said this, it's really important to make the recipes work for you. So feel free to swap out or add ingredients to suit your family. It makes me really happy to hear how people have adapted my recipes. Not only because it gives me ideas(!) but because, if you've made it work for you, you will probably keep cooking it.

Most of the dishes in this book are created for four people. We are a family of four so it made sense to make the recipes with this quantity in mind. You can obviously scale down all of the recipes to feed two, or even better, stick with what is listed and freeze half for another day!

a note on FISH

I use a mix of fresh and frozen fish depending on where I buy my ingredients and what is on offer that week. As long as they are thoroughly defrosted you can use either. However, I try to use frozen where possible as it tends to be cheaper and you can defrost what you need for that recipe, and save the rest for another time.

SHOPPING *on a budget*

I nearly didn't include this section in the book. I was worried that I might sound a bit preachy about shopping on a budget. Especially when I have weeks myself where my food recycling is overflowing and meal planning is thin on the ground! This list is a useful reminder to me.

It is so hard when life is busy to pay attention to your supermarket shop. Let's face it, it's boring. But making just a couple of changes will have a big impact on your weekly spend. These are some of the rules I try to live by:

BUY FROZEN AND TINNED FRUIT AND VEG
They cost less and are just as good for you (so long as they're not packed in juices with added sugar). They won't go off as quickly and, with frozen vegetables, you can simply use as much as you need.

SWITCH BRANDS
It sounds obvious, but we get very used to buying the same brands every week. Try swapping some of your branded items for 'own' brands. Some of the savings are huge!

PAY ATTENTION TO PRICES
We can get so used to our regular supermarket that we often don't check the prices. Check the cost of everything you put in your trolley – you may change your mind about some items!

SET A BUDGET AND TRY TO STICK TO IT
I know that it's easier said than done but when you focus on a maximum spend, it's amazing how much you will realise you don't need!

PLAN YOUR MEALS
Choose seven dinners and seven lunches that you are going to eat that week and write your weekly shopping list around them. It's difficult to plan for more than a week ahead and you'll usually end up spending more money doing 'top-up shops' if you do. Think little and often.

MAKE YOUR OWN LUNCH
It's really hard to find affordable food on the go, so make your own to take to work. Packed lunches are cheaper, healthier and a good way to use up leftovers.

MAKE EXTRA PORTIONS OF FOOD
That way, you can freeze portions, so you aren't tempted to buy expensive ready meals on nights when you're too busy to cook.

GO VEGETARIAN
Veggie meals are usually significantly cheaper than cuts of meat. Try going meat free at least one day a week.

KEEP A NOTE OF THE FOOD YOU'RE THROWING AWAY EACH WEEK
It's easy to buy things out of habit without noticing that it's never used. If you're throwing away the same things – stop buying them!

.AVE A PLAN FOR EVERYTHING YOU BUY
Don't buy food just because it's on offer. When you write your meal plan, try to think about ingredients that might be left over and what recipe would use them up.

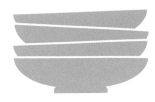

ESSENTIAL *ingredients*

There are a few staple ingredients that you will find you need to use for most recipes in one form or another, so I have included some notes about the herbs, spices and oils that I use most often, all of which are available from most discount supermarkets.

HERBS AND SPICES

Herbs and spices are one of the keys to great-tasting food. You should become familiar with using a good selection of fresh herbs:
- Basil
- Coriander
- Dill
- Mint
- Parsley
- Rosemary
- Thyme

As well as dried herbs and spices:
- Basil
- Mixed herbs
- Oregano
- Parsley
- Sage
- Thyme
- Chilli powder
- Ground cinnamon/Cinnamon sticks
- Ground cumin
- Ground coriander
- Ground ginger
- Paprika
- Turmeric

During the warmer months of the year, I buy fresh herb pots and plant them in containers outside. It's really easy to do and it ensures that you have the right herb whenever you need it. To re-pot a fresh herb plant, just fill a larger plant pot that has drainage holes in the bottom with soil and make a well in the middle that's large enough for the plant. Fresh herbs tend to be a little root bound. To ensure their success, tip the herb out of the container it came in and soak the roots in water for a couple of hours. Once done, gently break the roots up a little with your hands. Push the plant into the hole in the soil and cover the roots up with more earth. Water well and they should flourish!

a note about CURRY POWDER

Three of the recipes in this book require curry powder, which can be a little hard to come by in some discount supermarkets. However, they do sell the dried spices that you need to make your own curry powder blend:

- 4 tsp ground coriander
- 2 tsp turmeric
- 2 tsp chilli powder
- 1 tsp ground cumin
- ½ tsp ground ginger

Simply blend all of the spices together and store in an airtight container for up to three years. This will make a hot curry powder. If you want to make it mild to medium in heat, halve the amount of chilli powder.

OILS

You will notice that all of my recipes that require some form of frying will call for olive oil. It is the only oil that I use. It was once thought that olive oil was unsuitable for frying, and that bringing it to a high temperature made it in some way unhealthy. This is a myth. Olive oil is, in fact, one of the healthiest oils you can cook with. Processed vegetable oils are unnatural, and evidence has shown that over time they can cause harm. You can obviously use whatever oil you choose, but I would recommend giving olive oil a try. It is a little more expensive than other oils, but you don't need to use as much, so it will last longer. You can use either extra virgin olive oil or regular olive oil. Extra virgin olive oil is often more expensive though, so tends to be saved for dressings and marinades.

KITCHEN KIT

I have a very straightforward kitchen set-up. The fanciest pieces of kit that I own are a food processor and a potato ricer. I have a large, non-stick frying pan that I use for most things – from spaghetti bolognese to frying an egg. A good-quality griddle pan is a great investment; it is the only thing that I use for frying steaks and vegetables.

the savvy shopper's guide to
DISCOUNT SUPERMARKETS

TROLLEYS

To keep costs down and prevent trolleys going missing, discount supermarket trolleys require a coin to operate them, which will be refunded when you return the trolley after your shopping trip. So, you need to remember to bring your coin!

BRANDS

You will find some recognisable brands, along with plenty of new ones that you may not have seen before. I have yet to try something new that wasn't of great quality. Give them a go, as that is often where the real savings lie.

CHOICE

Newbie discount supermarket shoppers are often worried about the reduced choice of individual products – I know I was. That is until you realise you can live without having to choose from 15 different types of ketchup and 120 flavours of soup! Shopping in a smaller store with fewer products takes half the time.

THE MIDDLE AISLE

Ah, the middle aisle! Every week the main discount supermarkets have a special range on sale in the middle aisle. One week it might be power tools, the next it could be camping equipment. That is why it's been known for someone to go in for bread and milk and leave with a candyfloss maker and a shed!

FRESH FRUIT AND VEG

Every week, the discount supermarkets have a selected number of fruit and veg on offer. I always try to incorporate these into meals, as they are often so cheap that it's impossible to say no to these offers!

CHECKOUTS

One way that discount supermarkets keep their costs down is by having fewer tills in their stores. There are no express or self-service checkouts, just a new way of packing shopping which allows customers to be served faster and avoids queues.

Here's how it happens: load your shopping onto the conveyor belt. (OK, so far so good!) When it's your turn, wheel your trolley to the end and turn it around to face the cashier, pushing it up against the end of the till. They will scan the food through, and you will load it straight into your trolley. That's right, no bags. Once you're done, you can load your shopping into bags on the large loading shelf in front of the tills. However, I never do this as I find it much quicker to load the shopping straight into my bags, which are laid out in the boot of my car.

PRICES

The first thing that you will notice is the prices. They really are as low as people say they are! There are a few special offers and price cuts on certain foods in certain weeks, but generally it's just everyday low prices. There are no 'buy one get one free' offers, and no '3 for 2'. You will not see special offers dangled in front of your trolley. You are free to shop without the need for a calculator!

Novices will need to look out for the product prices – they are usually above the items rather than below, which took me a bit of getting used to at first!

my discount SHOPPING LIST

I thought it would be useful to include a summary of the ingredients that I most regularly buy. This list also covers almost all of the ingredients you will need for the recipes in this book. They are not necessarily weekly staples, for example I won't buy every kind of meat and fish each week, but they are the ingredients that I use most often and that I find are the most versatile to keep mealtimes interesting.

FRESH FRUIT AND VEGETABLES

- ☐ Romaine lettuce
- ☐ Rocket
- ☐ Celery
- ☐ Spinach
- ☐ Butternut squash
- ☐ Spring onions
- ☐ Lemons
- ☐ Kale
- ☐ Cherry tomatoes
- ☐ Peppers
- ☐ Cucumber
- ☐ Baking potatoes
- ☐ Charlotte potatoes
- ☐ Ginger

- ☐ Garlic
- ☐ Onions
- ☐ Courgettes
- ☐ Chillies
- ☐ Limes
- ☐ Tenderstem broccoli
- ☐ Little Gem lettuce
- ☐ Blueberries
- ☐ Apples
- ☐ Bananas
- ☐ Green beans
- ☐ Asparagus tips
- ☐ Cauliflower

My extras

FISH AND MEAT

- ☐ Peppered mackerel fillets
- ☐ Smoked mackerel fillets
- ☐ Mackerel fillets
- ☐ Aberdeen Angus steak
- ☐ 28-day matured steak

- ☐ Chicken thighs
- ☐ Chicken breast fillets
- ☐ Pork loin steaks
- ☐ Chorizo
- ☐ Diced beef

STORE CUPBOARD

- ❏ Long grain rice
- ❏ Chicken/vegetable stock cubes
- ❏ Microwave basmati rice
- ❏ Extra virgin olive oil
- ❏ Dried spaghetti
- ❏ Tagliatelle
- ❏ Spicy couscous
- ❏ Medium egg noodles
- ❏ Eggs
- ❏ Farfalle pasta

TINS, TUBS AND JARS

- ❏ Mackerel fillets in olive oil
- ❏ Coconut milk
- ❏ Kidney beans
- ❏ Anchovies
- ❏ Passata
- ❏ Tinned plum tomatoes
- ❏ Sundried tomatoes
- ❏ Sardines
- ❏ Gherkins
- ❏ Tuna
- ❏ Chickpeas

SAUCES AND DRESSINGS

- ❏ Mayonnaise
- ❏ Dijon mustard
- ❏ Horseradish sauce
- ❏ Red pesto
- ❏ English mustard
- ❏ Balsamic vinegar
- ❏ Soy sauce
- ❏ Maple syrup
- ❏ Green pesto
- ❏ Marmite

DRIED HERBS AND SPICES

- ❏ Paprika
- ❏ Oregano
- ❏ Mixed herbs
- ❏ Sage
- ❏ Ground black pepper
- ❏ Chilli powder
- ❏ Cinnamon
- ❏ Ground cumin
- ❏ Turmeric
- ❏ Ground ginger

My extras

FROZEN

- ❏ Sweetcorn
- ❏ Green beans
- ❏ Quorn mince
- ❏ Salmon fillets
- ❏ Tuna steak
- ❏ White fish fillets – I often use basa or cod
- ❏ Quorn chicken pieces
- ❏ Quorn sausages

BAKING

- ❏ Cocoa powder
- ❏ Golden syrup
- ❏ Baking powder
- ❏ Honey
- ❏ Caster sugar
- ❏ Plain flour
- ❏ Self-raising flour
- ❏ Icing sugar
- ❏ Puff pastry
- ❏ Shortcrust pastry
- ❏ Dark/plain/milk chocolate
- ❏ Dried mixed berries
- ❏ Light brown sugar

DAIRY

- ❏ Feta
- ❏ Salted butter
- ❏ Single cream
- ❏ Crème fraîche
- ❏ Greek yoghurt
- ❏ Garlic and herb soft cheese
- ❏ Parmesan cheese
- ❏ Gorgonzola
- ❏ Goat's cheese
- ❏ Halloumi
- ❏ Mozzarella

BREAD

- ❏ Ciabatta rolls
- ❏ Pitta bread
- ❏ Garlic and coriander naan
- ❏ Tortilla wraps
- ❏ Multi-seed loaf

FRESH HERBS

- ❏ Basil
- ❏ Parsley
- ❏ Rosemary
- ❏ Thyme
- ❏ Dill
- ❏ Mint
- ❏ Coriander

My extras

one week MEAL PLAN

The key to getting the most out of the food you buy every week is to plan ahead and avoid waste. Make a meal plan and use this to write your shopping list. Leftovers make great lunches, so try and freeze them for another day – you'll be glad of them when you're short of time!

Monday

LUNCH
Mackerel Pâté on Toast
A really quick, tasty lunch. Take it to work in a jar and make extra to use later in the week on pasta or salad. *See page 74.*

DINNER
Butternut Squash Risotto
A real crowd-pleaser – perfect for your 'Meat Free Monday' dinner. Make extra for lunches later in the week. *See page 94.*

DESSERT
Earl Grey Malt Loaf
I always try to make a cake early in the week. It tends to last a few days and makes us all less sad that it's Monday! *See page 162.*

Tuesday

LUNCH
Carrot, Cucumber and Chilli Mint Salad
Add crumbled feta and croutons to this recipe for a healthy, satisfying lunch. *See page 57.*

DINNER
Couscous-coated Salmon with New Potatoes and Steamed Vegetables
Cook twice as much salmon and refrigerate for use later in the week. *See page 88.*

Wednesday

LUNCH
Smoked Mackerel Salad
Pile high your favourite cold veg and salad leaves. Add a flaked, smoked mackerel fillet and drizzle with leftover Mackerel Pâté.

DINNER
Sweetcorn Soup and Cheesy Herb Bread
So simple and filling. The herb bread recipe makes a large loaf, so you should have some leftover for lunches. *See pages 26 and 48.*

DESSERT
15-Minute Apple and Blackberry Crumbles
A fast and delicious mid-week pud! *See page 156.*

Thursday

LUNCH
Fiery Peanut and Honey Salmon Noodle Salad
Use the leftover couscous salmon and substitute it for the chicken in my noodle salad. *See page 125.*

DINNER
Risotto Balls with Salad
Press leftover Butternut Squash Risotto into walnut-sized balls. Roll in fresh breadcrumbs until coated and shallow-fry in olive oil for a couple of minutes, until browned all over and heated through.

Friday

LUNCH
Ham and Herb Bread Sandwiches
Cut leftover herb bread (see page 48) into slices, butter and add ham and lettuce for a truly delicious Friday sandwich!

DINNER
Spicy Breaded Chicken with Potato Wedges and Salad
Make a simple feast fit for a Friday! Make extra chicken to use in lunches over the weekend. *See page 118.*

DESSERT
Mixed Berry and White Chocolate Cookies
Our family has always had 'Friday Treats' – a way to make the day even more special! Bake these with the kids or when you get home from work for a great start to the weekend! *See page 166.*

Saturday

LUNCH
*Cheese and Basil
French Toast*
A great way to use up stale bread from the week to make a tasty brunch for the whole family! *See page 44.*

DINNER
*Sausage and Roasted
Vegetable Pilaf*
A hearty weekend meal, full of veg and plenty of flavour. *See page 132.*

Sunday

LUNCH
Spicy Chicken Wraps
Cut up leftover Spicy Breaded Chicken *(see page 118)* and add to tortilla wraps with some mayo, tomato and shredded lettuce.

DINNER
*Chicken, Potato and
Chorizo Traybake*
This is a big dinner that can feed many. Perfect if you have friends over or for leftovers during the week. Divide the surplus into portions before freezing. *See page 112.*

DESSERT
Peanut Butter Seed Balls
Make these easy seed balls on a Sunday night to use in lunches and for snacks during the week. *See page 153.*

CONVERSION TABLES

Conversions are approximate and have been rounded up or down. Follow one set of measurements only – do not mix metric and imperial.

WEIGHTS

METRIC	IMPERIAL
15g	½oz
25g	1oz
40g	1½oz
50g	2oz
75g	3oz
100g	4oz
150g	5oz
175g	6oz
200g	7oz
225g	8oz
250g	9oz
275g	10oz
350g	12oz
375g	13oz
400g	14oz
425g	15oz
450g	1lb
550g	1¼lb
675g	1½lb
900g	2lb
1.5kg	3lb
1.75kg	4lb
2.25kg	5lb

VOLUME

METRIC	IMPERIAL
25ml	1floz
50ml	2fl oz
85ml	3fl oz
150ml	5fl oz (¼ pint)
300ml	10fl oz (½ pint)
450ml	15fl oz (¾ pint)
600ml	1 pint
700ml	1¼ pints
900ml	1½ pints
1 litre	1¾ pints
1.2 litres	2 pints
1.25 litres	2¼ pints
1.5 litres	2½ pints
1.6 litres	2¾ pints
1.75 litres	3 pints
1.8 litres	3¼ pints
2 litres	3½ pints
2.1 litres	3¾ pints
2.25 litres	4 pints
2.75 litres	5 pints
3.4 litres	6 pints
3.9 litres	7 pints
5 litres	8 pints (1 gal)

MEASUREMENTS

METRIC	IMPERIAL
0.5cm	¼ in
1cm	½ in
2.5cm	1 in
5cm	2 in
7.5cm	3 in
10cm	4 in
15cm	6 in
18cm	7 in
20cm	8 in
23cm	9 in
25cm	10 in
30cm	12 in

OVEN TEMPERATURES

140°C	275°F	Gas mark 1	200°C	400°F	Gas mark 6
150°C	300°F	Gas mark 2	220°C	425°F	Gas mark 7
160°C	325°F	Gas mark 3	230°C	450°F	Gas mark 8
180°C	350°F	Gas mark 4	240°C	475°F	Gas mark 9
190°C	375°F	Gas mark 5			

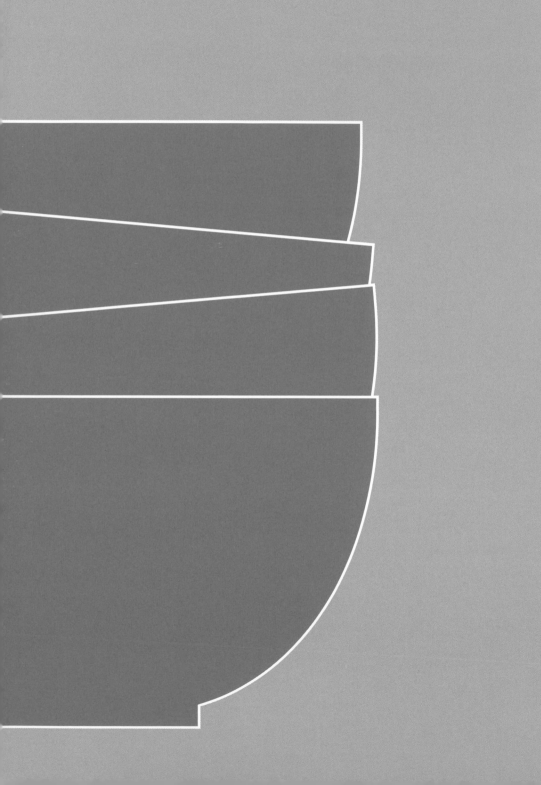

1

SOUPS AND SNACKS

Most of the meals in this chapter can be made in less than 20 minutes – and some in less than 10. They are perfect for lunches or light dinners, when you don't want to eat a mountain of food or when you can't face a long prep time.

SWEETCORN SOUP

This really is one of the easiest soups that you will ever make. Buttery, sweet and creamy, this makes the most of the wonderful flavours of sweetcorn. This is often on the menu when we have run out of food – I can nearly always get my hands on some frozen corn and a potato! The cream is optional, but it definitely adds richness.

MAKES 4 MUGS   ❄ **FREEZABLE**

1 onion, finely sliced
Butter, for frying
1 tsp finely chopped
    fresh rosemary
1 tsp finely chopped fresh
    thyme leaves (plus
    extra for garnish)
1 baking potato (approx
    300g/11oz), peeled and
    cut into 2cm/¾in cubes
200g/7oz frozen sweetcorn
    (no need to defrost)
1 litre/1¾ pints chicken stock
50ml/2fl oz single
    cream (optional)

Fry the onion in a large pan with a knob of butter for 10 minutes on a low heat. For the last 2 minutes of frying, add the chopped rosemary and thyme to soften them. Add the potato, sweetcorn and stock to the saucepan and stir well, then simmer for 20 minutes on a low heat, or until the potatoes are tender, stirring occasionally.

Once the soup is cooked, using a hand blender, blitz the soup until it's smooth, then pass the soup through a sieve to remove any sweetcorn kernels that the blender may have missed.

Return the soup to the pan, add the cream and extra thyme, if using, and gently warm through on the hob.

MARMITE BROTH

When I was little, my mum would make a variation of this recipe whenever she was on a diet. I can still remember the rich, almost beefy smell of this broth bubbling on the hob. Marmite has now been declared a 'Superfood', so it's time to bring this recipe back! High in B vitamins, low in calories and gluten-free, it makes the perfect snack.

 FEEDS 2   ❄ **FREEZABLE**

2 tsp Marmite
½ tsp ground black pepper
½ tsp chilli powder
1 tsp finely chopped thyme
250ml/8fl oz boiling water
Toast soldiers, to serve

Put the Marmite, pepper, chilli powder and thyme into a saucepan, add the boiling water and stir until the Marmite has melted. Simmer on a low heat for 5 minutes, until the water has absorbed the flavour of the herbs and spices. Serve piping hot in a mug with some toast soldiers on the side.

REALLY SUPER NOODLES

This is my take on a popular noodle brand. Before we had kids, my husband and I used to be big fans of packet noodles. There is just something so very satisfying about them. This homemade, chicken-flavoured version is as quick to make and as good to eat as its packet inspiration.

 FEEDS 2

350ml/12fl oz boiling water
1 tsp chopped fresh thyme
1 tsp dried sage
1 tsp dried mixed herbs
2 tsp chicken gravy
½ tsp salt
Freshly ground black pepper
Splash of soy sauce
2 nests of dried medium
    egg noodles (approx
    120g/4½oz)

To make the stock, mix the boiling water with the fresh and dried herbs, chicken gravy, salt, pepper and soy sauce.

Place the egg noodles in a saucepan and pour over the stock, then simmer, covered, for 5 minutes on a low heat, stirring occasionally. The noodles should absorb most of the stock so no need to drain before serving.

RED PEPPER HOUMOUS CRISPBREADS

Once a week I spend the day cleaning the house. It's not a job I enjoy, so I always make these as something to look forward to between chores – they are so tasty, you won't want them to end. Crispbreads are widely available from all supermarkets; use your favourite flavour or brand for this super speedy lunch.

MAKES 4 LOADED CRISPBREADS

200g/7oz tub of red pepper houmous (you are unlikely to use the whole tub unless feeding lots of people!)
4 crispbreads
80g/3oz feta cheese
Large handful of rocket leaves
8 cherry tomatoes, halved
Drizzle of balsamic vinegar
Freshly ground black pepper

Spread a thick layer of houmous on the underside of the crackers – the seeds make it hard to spread. Crumble the feta cheese evenly over the four crackers, then scatter over the rocket leaves and top with the cherry tomato halves. Finally, drizzle over a little balsamic vinegar and finish with a generous grind of black pepper.

RED PESTO, SPINACH AND RED PEPPER PASTA

Red pesto is one of my favourite ingredients. It is a pesto made with sundried tomatoes, so it's rich and packed full of flavour. It makes the perfect base for sauces and goes really well with the creamy soft cheese here. The kids love this for lunch. I tend to blend the sauce to hide some of the veg, but you can leave it chunky if you prefer more texture.

FEEDS 4

300g/11oz fusilli pasta
3 spring onions, roughly
    chopped into 5cm lengths
1 garlic clove, finely sliced
½ red pepper, deseeded
    and sliced
Olive oil, for frying
100g/4oz red pesto
    (roughly half a jar)
Handful of spinach leaves
1 tbsp water
125g/4½oz soft cheese

Put the pasta in a large saucepan of boiling, salted water and simmer for 10 minutes until it is tender.

While the pasta cooks, fry the spring onions, garlic and red pepper in a frying pan with a drizzle of olive oil on a low heat for 5 minutes.

Add the pesto, spinach, water and soft cheese to the frying pan, stir well then simmer on a low heat for 2 minutes, until the spinach is soft. Using a hand blender, whizz the sauce until smooth.

When the pasta is cooked, drain it, tip it into the pan of sauce and mix well. Heat through briefly and serve immediately.

SPICY TUNA MELT

There are many variations of this classic American diner dish. This one uses spicy Cheddar instead of Swiss cheese. If you can find pre-sliced spicy cheese, it makes this even quicker! If you want to reduce the amount of bread you're eating, just serve it as an open sandwich, leaving off the top slice of bread.

MAKES 2 SANDWICHES

4 slices of a multi-seed loaf
160g/5½oz tin of
    tuna, drained
2 tbsp mayonnaise
1 tsp Dijon mustard
½ tsp chilli powder
½ tsp freshly ground
    black pepper
Butter, for spreading
2 tomatoes, sliced
4 spicy cheese slices
4 Little Gem lettuce leaves

Put the slices of bread under a medium grill and toast until browned on one side.

Mix together the tuna, mayonnaise, Dijon mustard, chilli powder and ground black pepper.

Butter the toasted sides of the four pieces of bread. Divide the tuna mixture between two of the four slices, spreading it evenly over the toasted side.

Lay the tomato slices over the tuna, top with 2 slices of spicy cheese and put the remaining slice of bread on top of each – untoasted side up – to make a sandwich.

Grill each side of the sandwich until the bread is toasted and the cheese has melted.

Open up each sandwich and add a couple of lettuce leaves, then close up and serve immediately.

SPICY COUSCOUS PITTA BREADS

There was a time when I would eat couscous for lunch almost every day. Working from home, it's very hard to eat healthily and not to snack. Even a small amount of couscous seems to fill me up until dinner time – which keeps me away from the fridge! This is a healthy and satisfying lunch that's ready in 10 minutes.

FEEDS 2

100g/4oz pack spicy couscous
165ml/5½fl oz boiling water
2 pitta breads (I use
    wholemeal)
1 carrot
½ cucumber
6 sundried tomatoes from a jar,
    drained and finely chopped
30g/1oz feta, crumbled
Drizzle of olive oil
Salt and freshly ground
    black pepper

Put the couscous into a bowl and pour over the boiling water. Cover the bowl with cling film and leave for 10 minutes.

Using a knife, cut the pitta breads in half and make a pocket in each of them – making sure you go as close as you can to the edges.

Peel the carrot and cucumber, discard the skin and then, using a vegetable peeler, slice the carrot and cucumber into ribbons. Discard the inner cores of the vegetables.

When the couscous is ready, add the sundried tomatoes, carrot, cucumber, crumbled feta cheese and a drizzle of olive oil, and season with salt and pepper.

Mix everything together with your hands and divide the couscous between the pitta breads, pressing the mixture in gently.

CHEESY ASPARAGUS AND BROCCOLI WHEELS

I will admit that these wheels take a little longer to make than the other recipes in this chapter. However, they are good fun to cook and they taste amazing. You can serve them at a lunch, buffet or picnic, as they're great hot or cold.

MAKES 10 WHEELS

FREEZABLE

Olive oil, for frying
    and greasing
1 sheet of ready-rolled
    puff pastry
Plain flour, for dusting
5 tsp green pesto
5 tsp double cream
    or crème fraîche
1 head of broccoli,
    broken into florets
100g/4oz asparagus tips
50g/2oz Parmesan
    cheese, grated
Salt and freshly ground
    black pepper
1 egg yolk, beaten, to glaze

Heat the oven to 180°C/350°F/Gas mark 4. Grease a baking sheet with oil.

Lay the pastry on a lightly floured surface. Mix the pesto and cream or crème fraîche together, then spread it evenly over the pastry.

In a griddle or frying pan, heat some olive oil and fry the broccoli and asparagus for 15 minutes until slightly browned and tender. Leave to cool.

Using a sharp, heavy knife, cut the asparagus and broccoli into roughly 1cm/½in pieces, then dot them evenly over the pastry, followed by the Parmesan cheese and some salt and pepper.

With the short end facing you, loosely roll up the pastry like a Swiss roll. Using a pastry brush, glaze the outside of the pastry roll with the beaten egg yolk.

Cut the roll into 10 equal pieces. Gently separate the pieces and reshape them slightly as the process of cutting them will have squashed them a little. Place on the greased tray and bake for 20–25 minutes.

CARAMELISED ONION AND GOAT'S CHEESE TART

Caramelised onion, thyme and goat's cheese are a wonderful combination. This is a great picnic standby or tasty lunch. I always serve it with rocket leaves dressed with a little balsamic vinegar. The tart freezes really well, so you can prepare it the day before you want to serve it, put it in the freezer and bake when you're ready to eat it. You could also make little individual tarts.

MAKES 12 SLICES

FREEZABLE

Olive oil, for frying
    and greasing
2 large onions (red or white),
    cut in half and thinly sliced
3 tbsp honey
1 tsp soy sauce
1 tsp chopped fresh
    thyme leaves
1 tsp freshly ground
    black pepper
1 sheet of ready-rolled
    puff pastry
150g/5oz log goat's
    cheese, thinly sliced

Heat the oven to 200°C/400°F/Gas mark 6. Grease two baking sheets.

Heat the olive oil in a large frying pan and fry the onions over a low heat for 20 minutes, until softened. Add the honey, soy, thyme and pepper and stir for a further 10 minutes on low. Add 1 tablespoon of cold water to the hot pan and stir, mixing in all of the juices from the base of the pan. Take off the heat and leave to cool.

Slice the pastry sheet in half lengthways and put one piece on each baking sheet. Lightly score a line 5cm/2in in from the edge around each sheet to create a border. Divide the onion mixture evenly between the pastry sheets and spread within the border, to allow the pastry to puff up around the edge. Lay the goat's cheese slices at intervals over both pastries and bake for 25 minutes, until cooked and golden.

NAAN BREAD PIZZAS

This is a really tasty, quick way to make a lunchtime pizza, or in fact any time you don't fancy making a base. If you have kids, this is a great recipe to wheel out when they have friends over. A naan bread each and a few toppings to choose from and they can make their own dinner! I have included my favourite toppings opposite.

MAKES 2 PIZZAS   ❄ **FREEZABLE**

4 tbsp passata
Pack of 2 naan bread (plain
   or garlic and coriander)
60g/2½oz Cheddar
   cheese, grated
1 tsp dried oregano

Spread 2 tablespoons of passata over each naan bread, making sure you go right up to the edges, then add your preferred topping (see opposite).

Cover the topping with Cheddar cheese and sprinkle over the oregano. Cook under a medium grill for 5 minutes, or until the cheese has melted and the naan is becoming crisp.

Spinach and Anchovy

Drain a 50g/2oz tin of anchovies. Slice each fillet into roughly 4 pieces. Put 50g/2oz of spinach into boiling, salted water for 1 minute, then drain and squeeze out the excess water. Arrange the anchovies and spinach evenly over the passata on 2 naan breads and cover in Cheddar cheese before grilling.

Sundried Tomato and Goat's Cheese

Finely slice 8 drained sundried tomatoes into slithers and arrange them over the passata on 2 naan breads. Slice 100g/4oz goat's cheese into discs and place them over the sundried tomatoes. Sprinkle over a little Cheddar, just to fill the gaps between the goat's cheese, and grill for 5 minutes.

Feta, Rocket and Courgette

Cut the ends off a courgette and thinly slice it lengthways. Place the courgette in a hot pan and fry in olive oil on both sides until slightly coloured and soft. Arrange the courgette slices over the naans. Sprinkle 50g/2oz crumbled feta and 25g/1oz Parmesan oven the naans and grill. Scatter over a handful of rocket and drizzle with balsamic vinegar before serving.

Chorizo, Grilled Peppers and Mozzarella

Chop a whole mozzarella ball into thin circles and divide between two naan breads. Next, slice 16 thin discs from a chorizo sausage and divide them between the naan breads. Add thinly sliced strips of grilled peppers from a jar and bake for 10–15 minutes in an oven preheated to 200°C/400°F/Gas mark 6, until the chorizo is cooked through and the naan is crisp.

Prosciutto, Chicken and Basil

Sprinkle some Cheddar cheese over the passata sauce on 2 naan breads. Arrange 4 slices of prosciutto across each of the naan, and place some small pieces of cooked roast chicken breast in between. Bake in an oven preheated to 200°C/400°F/Gas mark 6 for 10–15 minutes, until the chicken and prosciutto are cooked through. Finish with some finely chopped fresh basil.

CUBAN SANDWICH

This famous American sandwich originated in Florida and later became one of Miami's most popular fast foods. Unfortunately, not all of the ingredients in a traditional Cuban sandwich are readily available in all countries. Discount supermarkets have a great selection of cold meats, though, so I have found some substitutes that make my version of this sandwich taste like the real thing! All of the ingredients are essential to the flavour, so don't leave anything out!

MAKES 2 SANDWICHES

Pack of 2 ciabatta rolls
Dijon mustard, for spreading
Mayonnaise, for spreading
4 slices of roast pork loin
4 slices of smoked ham
4 slices of Emmental cheese
2 gherkins
2 tsp melted butter

Slice open the ciabatta rolls horizontally and spread a thin layer of mustard on the bottom halves of each. Then spread mayonnaise on the top halves.

Fill each sandwich with a slice of pork, followed by a slice of ham and then a slice of cheese. Top with some sliced chilli gherkins, then pop on the top half of the roll and press down firmly with your hand.

Using a pastry brush, coat both the top and bottom of the sandwiches in the melted butter. Put the sandwiches in a griddle or frying pan set over a medium heat. Toast on one side, then turn and cook on the other side. These sandwiches burn easily, so keep a close eye on them and add some oil to the pan if it gets too dry. You may need to turn the sandwiches a few times until the bread is crisp and golden brown and the cheese has started to melt. Slice in half and serve hot.

CHEESE AND BASIL FRENCH TOAST

If it's comfort food you're after, look no further. This is a firm favourite with my family and perfect on a lazy Sunday morning. It's also a really good recipe for using up stale bread – if the bread is too fresh it can get a little soggy as it absorbs too much of the egg mixture. Try using French bread or crumpets, too, if you have some left over.

 FEEDS 2

2 eggs
40g/1½oz Cheddar
    cheese, grated
3 tbsp milk
1 tsp finely chopped basil
Butter, for frying
2 slices of bread, cut in
    half on the diagonal
Salt and freshly ground
    black pepper

Beat the eggs with the grated cheese, milk, basil and some salt and pepper to taste.

Heat a knob of butter in a frying pan or griddle.

Soak each piece of bread in the egg mixture for a few seconds. Use your hands to make sure both sides of the bread are covered in egg and cheese. Fry the bread in the pan for 2–3 minutes on each side, until golden brown and crispy.

2

SIDES AND SALADS

Side dishes and salads can sometimes be the best part of the meal. A roast dinner is a great example of this; the meat is often just a vehicle for the many accompaniments that make this meal special. It's easy to get stuck in a rut with sides, though, so give some of these a try and beef up your repertoire.

CHEESY HERB BREAD

When I was young, my mum made lots of soups and she would always bake herb bread to serve with it. The smell of this loaf baking takes me right back to childhood. Mum's original herb bread recipe has been lost for many years, but this is an excellent replica. It is basically a giant cheese scone, and you can use any cheese that you might have in the fridge, such as Stilton or brie. Serve big, buttered wedges of this bread with soup.

 FEEDS 4

❄ **FREEZABLE**

140g/4½oz butter, plus
    extra for greasing
560g/1¼lb self-raising flour,
    plus extra for dusting
1 tsp baking powder
1 tsp salt
1 tbsp dried mixed herbs
100g/4oz cheese (I use
    50g/2oz Wensleydale and
    50g/2oz mature Cheddar)
375ml/13fl oz milk

Heat the oven to 200°C/400°F/Gas mark 6. Grease a large baking tray.

In a large mixing bowl, rub the butter into the flour, until it resembles breadcrumbs. Add the baking powder, salt and mixed herbs and ensure they are all mixed together. Crumble or cut the cheese into small chunks, add to the bowl and mix well.

Make a well in the middle of the dry ingredients and pour in the milk. Using your hands, blend the mixture into a dough and lightly knead it on a floured surface.

Form the dough into a large ball, then gently flatten the top so that it is a flat circle roughly 5cm/2in thick – it will rise in the oven! Bake for 50–60 minutes.

Remove from the oven and allow to cool a little before cutting.

CHEESE, POTATO AND ONION ROSTI

Cheese, potato and onion are a combination I will never tire of. This is a great lunchtime recipe as it's so quick to make. Add a poached egg and some wilted spinach to make a hearty meal of it.

MAKES 6 ROSTI

FREEZABLE

2 large baking potatoes
1 onion
1 egg, beaten
100g/4oz mature Cheddar
    cheese, grated
Olive oil, for frying
Salt and freshly ground
    black pepper

Coarsely grate the potatoes, with skins on, and then use your hands to squeeze out any excess moisture. Coarsely grate the onion. Put the onion and potato in a mixing bowl and stir in the beaten egg, grated cheese and seasoning.

Divide the mixture into 6 and press each rosti firmly between your hands, again squeezing out any moisture.

Cook the rosti in olive oil in a large frying pan on a medium heat for 3 minutes on each side, until they are a lovely brown colour and cooked through.

COURGETTE, FETA AND CHILLI

This simple, colourful and tasty dish is the perfect way to make courgettes the star of the show. This salad is great at a summer barbecue, or served with grilled fish or chicken during the warmer months.

 FEEDS 4

3 courgettes
Olive oil, for frying
1 garlic clove, finely chopped
2 red chillies, deseeded
    and finely chopped
100g/4oz feta cheese
Salt and freshly ground
    black pepper

Remove the ends of the courgettes, then, leaving the skin on, slice them lengthways about 0.5cm/¼in thick – you should get 5–6 slices out of each courgette.

Heat a small amount of olive oil in a griddle or frying pan. Put half of the courgettes in the pan, with half of the garlic and chilli, and fry for 2 minutes on each side.

Remove the courgettes, garlic and chilli from the pan and put them on some kitchen paper to remove excess oil. Cook the remaining courgettes in the same way.

Put the courgettes, chilli and garlic on a plate, season with salt and pepper and crumble feta cheese over the top. Serve while still warm.

ROASTED LETTUCE

I nearly didn't include this dish in the book – it's so simple it can't really be described as a recipe! However, I love this salad, especially with fish, and it's nice to do something else with lettuce, particularly when the weather gets colder. You can use an oil-based salad dressing instead of olive oil if you prefer.

 FEEDS 4

2 romaine lettuces
1 tbsp olive oil
1 tbsp balsamic vinegar
½ tsp chilli flakes
Salt and freshly ground
    black pepper

Heat the oven to 200°C/400°F/Gas mark 6.

Cut each lettuce in half lengthways, leaving the tough end on to hold the lettuce together. Place them, cut side up, on a baking tray.

Mix the olive oil, balsamic vinegar and chilli flakes together and pour over the lettuce. Use your hands to coat the lettuces all over and season with salt and pepper. Bake in the oven for 10 minutes, until they are soft and browning.

CARROT, CUCUMBER AND CHILLI MINT SALAD

This is my salad of the summer; I eat it virtually every day when the weather is hot. The crunch of the vegetables combined with the chilli and mint make it very refreshing. You can use olive oil rather than the oil from a sundried tomato jar if you prefer, but the tomato flavour definitely adds to the dish. If you crumble some feta over the top and add some croutons, it's a lunch all on its own!

 FEEDS 2

2 carrots
1 cucumber
½ red chilli, deseeded
    and finely chopped
8 mint leaves, finely chopped
1 tbsp oil from a jar of
    sundried tomatoes
Salt and freshly ground
    black pepper

Using a vegetable peeler, peel the carrots and discard the skin. Working around the carrots, use the peeler to slice them into even-sized ribbons; discard the core when you reach it. Do the same with the cucumber, but this time use the skin, then discard the cucumber's mushy core.

Combine the chilli and the mint leaves with the oil, then season with salt and pepper.

Pour the dressing over the carrot and cucumber and use your hands to mix together until all the vegetables are coated.

CUCUMBER AND MINT RAITA RICE SALAD

I have always loved raita; the lovely cool, refreshing flavours of yoghurt, mint and cucumber work perfectly with spicy food. This recipe just takes those ingredients and makes them into a more substantial salad dish. I usually serve this with meat or fish, but it would work well with a curry. If you like a bit of heat, add some finely sliced chilli as a garnish.

 FEEDS 4

280g/10oz microwave
    basmati rice
1 heaped tbsp Greek yoghurt
½ cucumber, chopped
    into small chunks
10 mint leaves, finely chopped,
    plus a few extra to garnish
Salt and freshly ground
    black pepper

Microwave the rice for 2 minutes according to the packet instructions. Tip out the cooked rice into a mixing bowl, cool to room temperature, then cover with cling film and place in the fridge until cold.

In a separate bowl, mix together the Greek yoghurt, cucumber and mint leaves.

Add the dressing to the cold rice and combine. Season with salt and pepper and serve immediately, garnished with a few extra mint leaves, or store in the fridge in a covered container.

ROAST POTATO AND HALLOUMI SALAD WITH BALSAMIC GLAZE

This is much simpler than it appears and is well worth the effort. It really does taste as good as it looks. The vibrant colours of the peppers and broccoli and the textures of the potatoes and cheese make this the perfect summer dish. I always make it when we have a barbecue. Serve it on a platter and it makes a great centrepiece!

FEEDS 4–6 AS A STARTER OR A SIDE

300g/11oz Charlotte
    potatoes, cut in half
Olive oil, for roasting
2 red peppers, deseeded
    and cut into chunks
100g/4oz tenderstem broccoli,
    thick stems removed
225g/8oz halloumi,
    thickly sliced
2 Little Gem lettuces
3 radishes, finely sliced
Mayonnaise (optional)
Salt and freshly ground
    black pepper

FOR THE BALSAMIC GLAZE
200ml/7fl oz balsamic vinegar
50ml/2fl oz water
40g/1½oz light brown sugar

Heat the oven to 220°C/425°F/Gas mark 7.

Place the potatoes in a saucepan and cover them with cold, salted water. Bring to the boil and simmer for 10 minutes. Drain, then put them in a roasting tin and, using a fork, gently break them up into smaller pieces. Drizzle them with olive oil and use your hands to ensure that they are all coated. Season with salt and pepper. Roast in the oven for 20–30 minutes, until crisp and brown.

While the potatoes are roasting, make the balsamic glaze. Mix the balsamic vinegar with the water and sugar and pour into a pan. Gently bring it to the boil. Turn down the heat and simmer for 10 minutes until the liquid has reduced by roughly half. Leave to cool.

Fry the peppers, broccoli and halloumi in a griddle together with a little oil, turning regularly, for about 10 minutes. The halloumi will take a little less time.

Arrange the lettuce leaves over a large plate. Arrange the radish slices over the top. Add the roast potatoes, halloumi, broccoli and peppers. Season; be generous with the black pepper.

Dress the salad with balsamic glaze and mayonnaise, if you like.

MUSTARD AND HONEY GREEN BEAN SALAD

I like to have a few easy salads up my sleeve for those warmer months. This is one of my favourites. It goes really well with chicken or fish and the flavour of mustard is mild, so the kids like it too. I usually serve it when we have friends over for a barbecue, but it works just as well as a midweek staple.

 FEEDS 4

225g/8oz green beans
160g/5¼oz sugar snap peas
25g/1oz butter
1 tsp honey
2 tsp Dijon mustard
Salt and freshly ground
    black pepper

Put the green beans and sugar snap peas into a saucepan and cover with boiling water. Simmer for 15 minutes, until they are tender.

In a separate saucepan, melt the butter then add the honey, mustard and salt and pepper to the pan.

Drain the vegetables and place them in a serving bowl. Pour over the dressing and mix well so that the vegetables are thoroughly coated.

BACON, SPRING ONION AND SOURED CREAM POTATO SALAD

I love a potato salad! The bacon and spring onion gives this so much flavour and it's not swimming in sauce. It's perfect for a barbecue but it works well as a midweek meal with meat or fish.

 FEEDS 4

1kg/2lb 2oz bag of
    Charlotte potatoes
Drizzle of olive oil
Bunch of sliced spring onions,
    green and white parts
200g/7oz smoked bacon
    (cut into small pieces)
1 tsp paprika, plus
    extra to garnish
3 tbsp soured cream
Salt and freshly ground
    black pepper

Cut the potatoes in half, or cut larger potatoes into thirds, so that they are roughly equal in size. Place in a saucepan and cover with cold, salted water. Bring to the boil and simmer on a low heat for 20 minutes, or until the potatoes are tender.

In the meantime, heat some olive oil in a frying pan. Add the sliced spring onions, bacon and paprika. Fry on a medium heat for 5 minutes, until the bacon is crispy. Add the soured cream to the pan, mix well and season.

Drain the potatoes and mix with the dressing. Sprinkle a little paprika over the top and serve.

ICEBERG WEDGES WITH FETA DRESSING

This salad is a favourite of mine. The dry, salty flavour of the feta with the balsamic vinegar makes a sharp and rich combination. The toasted almonds add some sweetness and texture, so use them if you can. You can put this dressing on any lettuce or veg, but I think it works really well with iceberg because its high water content balances the dry flavours of the dressing.

FEEDS 4

1 iceberg lettuce
100g/4oz crumbled feta
25ml/1fl oz olive oil
25ml/1fl oz cold water
2 tsp balsamic vinegar
Pinch of lemon zest
Small handful of flaked
   almonds
1 radish, to garnish
Freshly ground black pepper

Cut the lettuce in half lengthways, leaving the rough stalk in place so that the lettuce holds together. Cut each half into thick wedges and place on a serving plate.

To make the dressing, put the feta, olive oil, water, balsamic vinegar and lemon zest in a bowl. Using a hand blender, mix until you have a smooth dressing. You can add a bit more water if you prefer your dressing a little runnier. Season with some ground black pepper (you won't need salt as feta is already salty).

Put the flaked almonds into a dry frying pan and fry on a medium heat for 2 minutes, until they are a lovely golden colour. Keep them moving in the pan so that they don't burn.

Spoon the dressing over the lettuce, sprinkle the toasted almonds and thinly sliced radish over the salad and serve.

MAIN MEALS

3
FISH

This chapter, probably more than any other in this book, uses the fewest ingredients. I have tried to make these dishes fresh and simple, so that the fish is the star of the show, getting the best out of the wonderful array of fish that is available in our discount supermarkets.

CRISPY FISH BITES

The batter in this recipe is much lighter than the version you find in a chip shop, as it uses sparkling water, giving it a tempura texture. These fish bites are shallow-fried instead of deep-fried so they absorb less fat. So you don't have to feel guilty about having a pile of chips with them!

 **FEEDS 4**

❄️ **FREEZABLE**

110g/4oz self-raising flour, plus extra for dusting the fish
1 tsp baking powder
½ tsp paprika
½ tsp chilli powder
½ tsp salt
Freshly ground black pepper
160ml/5fl oz sparkling water
400g/14oz bag of frozen basa fillets, defrosted (or another white fish of your choice)
Olive oil, for frying

Combine all of the dry ingredients – the flour, baking powder, paprika, chilli, salt and pepper – in a mixing bowl. Gradually add the sparkling water and gently whisk until the batter is smooth and lump-free.

Cut each of the defrosted basa fillets into 5 bite-sized pieces. Heat some olive oil, approximately 0.5cm/¼in deep, in a frying pan.

One at a time, roll each fish piece in the flour, then when coated, dip it into the flavoured batter. Put the fish straight into the hot pan and fry for 2 minutes each side, or until golden brown and crisp. Put the fish on a piece of kitchen paper to absorb the excess oil. Add more oil as and when required. Serve immediately.

FISHCAKES

Of all of the recipes in this book, I would say this one takes the longest time to make – not because it's complicated, but because it seems to create a lot of washing up! It is well worth it, though. Double up the ingredients to make extra and freeze them uncooked. They make a great standby.

MAKES 8 FISHCAKES

FREEZABLE

800g/1¾lb potatoes, peeled and chopped into chunks
380g/13oz bag of frozen basa or cod fillets, defrosted
600ml/1 pint cold milk
3 tbsp finely chopped fresh herbs (I use thyme, mint and dill)
Bunch of finely chopped spring onions (white and green parts)
100g/4oz tinned sweetcorn, drained
2 slices of bread, blitzed into crumbs
Olive oil, for frying
Salt and freshly ground black pepper
Lemon wedges to serve

Put the potatoes in a large saucepan and cover with cold, salted water. Bring the water to the boil and simmer on a low heat for 20 minutes, until the potatoes are tender. Drain the potatoes and mash until smooth.

While the potatoes are cooking, put the fish fillets into a separate saucepan and cover with cold milk. (You may need more or less milk than I have listed, depending on the size of saucepan.) Bring the milk slowly to the boil and simmer for 2 minutes. Remove the cooked fish from the milk and gently flake into a bowl.

Add the fish, herbs, spring onions and frozen sweetcorn to the mashed potato and season with salt and pepper. Mix thoroughly.

Divide the mixture into 8 and, using your hands, press them into fishcakes, then dip them into the breadcrumbs on both sides to ensure they are coated.

Heat the olive oil in a pan and shallow-fry for 3–4 minutes on each side until crisp and golden. Drain on kitchen paper before serving with lemon wedges.

SMOKED MACKEREL PÂTÉ

Looking at the list of ingredients below, this recipe shouldn't work – but it really does! The peppery flavour of the fish with the coolness of the crème fraîche is wonderful and the horseradish and Dijon give it a decent kick. This is quite a runny pâté – it's still thick enough to spread over toast, but it also works well as a salad dressing or as a sauce for pasta. You don't need much of it as it's very rich.

 FEEDS 4 (OR 2 SERVINGS AS PASTA SAUCE)

3 peppered smoked
    mackerel fillets
100g/4oz crème fraîche
1 tsp Dijon mustard
1 tsp horseradish sauce
Pinch of salt and freshly
    ground black pepper

Remove the skin from the mackerel fillets and break them into small flakes, then place them in a mixing bowl with the crème fraîche, mustard, horseradish, salt and pepper. Using a hand blender, mix everything together until smooth.

Transfer to a bowl, cover with cling film and place in the fridge for at least 30 minutes before serving.

SMOKED HADDOCK AND POTATO SOUP

In my opinion this is the best way to cook smoked haddock. The salty, smoky flavour of the fish combined with creamy potato and sweetcorn is wonderful. I can literally taste it now! Don't add any salt to the soup, as the fish brings enough.

 FEEDS 2

❄️ **FREEZABLE**

1 onion, finely chopped
25g/1oz butter
1 large potato, peeled and
    cut into 2cm/¾in dice
1 chicken stock cube
600ml/1 pint boiling water
2 smoked haddock fillets,
    skin removed and
    cut into chunks
100g/4oz frozen sweetcorn
50ml/2fl oz single cream
Freshly ground black pepper

Fry the onion in melted butter on a low heat for 5 minutes. Add the potato dice to the pan and continue to fry for a further 10 minutes, stirring regularly so that they don't stick.

Mix the stock cube with the boiling water until it's dissolved, then pour the stock into the pan along with the fish and sweetcorn and simmer for 10 minutes, until the potato is tender.

Just before serving, add the cream and pepper and gently heat through.

THREE WAYS WITH TINNED TUNA

**MAKES 4 LOADED
HALF POTATOES**

2 large baking potatoes
Olive oil, for drizzling
160g/5½oz tin of tuna,
    drained
2 tbsp mayonnaise
50g Cheddar cheese, grated
    (plus a little extra to
    sprinkle over the top)
1 tsp chives, finely chopped
Salt and freshly ground
    pepper

LOADED TUNA POTATO SKINS

Heat the oven to 200°C/400°F/Gas mark 6.

Pierce the potatoes several times with a sharp knife.
Microwave both of them on a high heat for 5–7 minutes
on each side or until soft, depending on the size of the
potatoes. Set aside until they are cool enough to handle.

Drizzle a little olive oil on each of the potatoes and, using
a pastry brush, spread it all over the skins. This will make
them go really crispy in the oven.

Cut both of the potatoes in half and place them on a
baking tray. Using a teaspoon, carefully scoop out the
filling without damaging the skins, and add it to a mixing
bowl. Add the tuna, mayonnaise, cheese, chives and
seasoning to the potato and mix well, slightly mashing
the potato as you stir.

Divide the mixture into 4 and press into each of the
potato skins, gently reshaping the potato in the process.
Add a little grated cheese to the top of each one and bake
in the oven for 30 minutes.

MAKES 8 RISSOLES

500g/1lb 2oz cold cooked rice
2 × 160g/5½oz tins of tuna,
    drained
½ courgette, roughly
    grated (skin left on)
2 tbsp tomato purée
85g/3oz frozen sweetcorn,
    defrosted
Salt and freshly ground pepper

TUNA RISSOLES

Add the rice, tuna, grated courgette, tomato purée,
sweetcorn, salt, pepper and basil to a large mixing bowl
and stir until all of the ingredients are combined and evenly
spread.

Put 1½ slices of bread into a food processor and blitz
to make breadcrumbs. Add the breadcrumbs to the
rice mixture and stir in, until you can no longer see the
breadcrumbs and the mixture is a little stiffer. Blitz the

6 basil leaves, finely chopped
3 slices of bread
2 tbsp olive oil, for frying

remaining bread in the food processor to make more breadcrumbs and place them on a clean worktop.

Divide the rice mixture into 8 equal-sized balls. Roll each ball between the palms of your hands, then coat in the breadcrumbs so it is completely covered. Gently press down on the top of the ball so that it resembles a fish cake. Cover the rissoles with cling film and place in the fridge for at least 30 minutes.

Heat the olive oil in a non-stick frying pan and add 3 or 4 of the rissoles to the pan at a time. Fry them gently for 3–4 minutes on each side, until they are golden brown and cooked through.

TINNED TUNA MEATBALLS

MAKES 16 BALLS, FEEDS 4   **FREEZABLE**

280g/10oz dried spaghetti

FOR THE MEATBALLS
2 × 160g/5½oz tins of tuna, drained
3 heaped tbsp green pesto
100g/4oz fresh breadcrumbs
1 egg, beaten
Olive oil, for frying

FOR THE SAUCE
1 onion, finely chopped
1 garlic clove, finely chopped
1 red pepper, deseeded and cut into small cubes
Olive oil, for drizzling
1 tsp sugar
2 tsp dried oregano
500g/1lb 2oz passata

Cook the spaghetti in a pan of boiling, salted water for 8 minutes, or until al dente.

Combine all of the meatball ingredients in a mixing bowl. Using your hands, press them into 16 equal-sized balls. Shallow-fry the meatballs in a pan with olive oil for about 5 minutes. Turn them regularly until they are crisp and browned all over.

Meanwhile, prepare the sauce. Put the onion, garlic and pepper in a frying pan, drizzle them in olive oil and fry on a low heat for 10 minutes, stirring occasionally. Add the sugar and oregano to the pan and fry for a further 2 minutes, then add the browned meatballs and the passata and simmer for 10 minutes, stirring regularly until the meatballs and sauce are heated through.

Drain the spaghetti, add to the meatballs and sauce, mix thoroughly and serve.

SALMON, POTATO AND DILL CRUMBLE

I think of salmon as a summer food, but this is a perfect autumn dinner. It not only gives you another way to eat salmon, but it manages to be both light and comforting at the same time. If you want to make this a little healthier, just leave out the cheese from the topping and use low-fat crème fraîche.

 **FEEDS 4**

❄️ **FREEZABLE**

300g/11oz Charlotte potatoes
4 salmon fillets (I use
    frozen wild pink salmon
    fillets, defrosted)
Bunch of spring onions,
    white and green parts
    finely chopped
30g/1¼oz spinach
200g/7oz crème fraîche
2 tsp finely chopped fresh dill
Zest of ½ lemon
2 slices of bread
100g/4oz Wensleydale
    or Cheddar cheese
Salt and freshly ground
    black pepper

Heat the oven to 180°C/350°F/Gas mark 4.

Cut each of the potatoes into quarters. Place in a pan and cover with cold, salted water and bring to the boil. Simmer on a medium heat for 10 minutes, until they are tender.

Cut the salmon steaks into bite-sized pieces. In an ovenproof pie dish, mix the salmon with the finely chopped spring onions, spinach, crème fraîche, 1 teaspoon of the finely chopped dill, the lemon zest and 2 tablespoons of water.

Drain the potatoes and add them to the salmon. Stir and season with salt and pepper.

Finely chop the bread, using a large heavy knife, into chunky breadcrumbs. Don't grate the bread, as the breadcrumbs will be too fine. Chop up the cheese to roughly the same size as the bread and combine the bread, cheese and remaining dill, then spread evenly over the salmon mixture. Cook for 40 minutes, until the top is golden brown.

CURRIED MACKEREL RICE WITH TOASTED ALMONDS

If I had to choose one meal to live on for the rest of my life, this would be it. When I was pregnant with my eldest son I was obsessed with eating oily fish every day. One day, I accidentally bought a tin of mackerel in curry sauce. I gave it a try and realised what a great combination it was!

 FEEDS 4

Olive oil, for frying
1 onion, sliced into half moons
50g/2oz curly kale
2 tins of mackerel
    fillets, drained
2 × 280g/10oz packets
    microwave basmati rice
1 tbsp curry powder
    (see page 12)
Handful of flaked almonds
Greek yoghurt, to serve

Heat the olive oil in a pan on a medium heat and fry the onion for 10 minutes, until softened. Add the kale and drizzle with a little more olive oil. Fry on a low heat for a further 5 minutes. Add the drained mackerel to the pan and gently flake the fish with a fork.

Cook the rice in the microwave according to packet instructions.

Add the rice and curry powder to the pan and turn up the heat, frying for 2 minutes while stirring. Add 2 tablespoons of cold water, picking up all the spices from the bottom of the pan and making the mixture a little looser. Mix well.

Place the flaked almonds in a separate frying pan and lightly toast them for 2 minutes.

Serve the rice sprinkled with the toasted almonds and with some Greek yoghurt on the side.

TUNA PESTO PASTA

I appreciate that the title of this dish sounds a little like a student dinner. In some ways it is – it's so simple! The tuna steaks give it a really meaty bite and the crème fraîche is lovely and creamy when combined with the pesto. I use farfalle or 'bow-tie' pasta, but you can use whichever pasta shape you like.

 **FEEDS 4**

250g/9oz dried farfalle pasta
4 frozen tuna steaks, defrosted
Olive oil, for frying
300g/11oz crème fraîche
190g/7oz jar of green pesto
150g/5oz frozen green beans

Put the pasta in a pan of boiling water and simmer for 10–15 minutes, until al dente.

In the meantime, cut the tuna steaks into 5 pieces per steak. Fry the tuna chunks in olive oil on a medium heat for 3 minutes, turning regularly to seal all over.

Add the crème fraîche and pesto to the pan, stir well and cook for 3 minutes, until heated through.

At the same time, put the green beans in a microwavable dish. Cover them in boiling water and microwave on full power for 5 minutes. Drain the beans and add to the pan with the pesto sauce.

Drain the pasta and add to the sauce. Stir well and gently heat through.

SARDINE BUTTER TAGLIATELLE WITH GARLIC BREADCRUMBS

I love this recipe. There is something very satisfying about making a healthy, filling meal from a cheap tin of fish! Sardines are packed full of vitamins and nutrients, some of which are hard to find in other foods. I use tagliatelle or spaghetti for this recipe but you could use any pasta. Make a batch of garlic breadcrumbs to freeze and you can add them to any rice or pasta dish.

 FEEDS 4

300g/11oz tagliatelle
2 × 125g/4½oz tins
   of sardines
50g/2oz butter
Squeeze of lemon juice
2 garlic cloves, finely chopped
2 slices of bread, whizzed
   into crumbs
Olive oil, for frying
Salt and freshly ground
   black pepper

Cook the tagliatelle in a pan of salted boiling water for 10 minutes, until al dente.

Place the sardines and butter into a bowl and mash them together until you have a smooth paste. Stir in the lemon juice and season with salt and pepper.

Mix the garlic with the breadcrumbs. Heat the oil in the pan and fry the breadcrumbs on a medium heat for 2–3 minutes, until crispy. Keep stirring them to prevent them burning.

Drain the pasta and put the sardine butter on top. Gently mix the butter into the pasta until it has all melted.

Serve the pasta topped with the garlic breadcrumbs.

SWEET CHILLI MACKEREL PASTA

If you want a tasty, simple and cheap way of getting more fish into your diet, look no further. This sauce can be knocked up in the time it takes you to boil the pasta. Smoked mackerel with sweet chilli sauce is a must try – it gives this dish a real kick and cuts through the crème fraîche.

 FEEDS 4

300g/11oz fusilli pasta
2 leeks, finely sliced
25g/1oz butter
3 smoked mackerel fillets,
  skin removed
300g/11oz crème fraîche
Salt and freshly ground
  black pepper
1 tsp chilli powder
5 tbs sweet chilli sauce

Cook the pasta in boiling, salted water for 10 minutes, until al dente. Drain.

Fry the leeks in melted butter in a pan on a low heat for 10 minutes, until soft. Add the chilli powder to the pan for two minutes at the end of frying.

Flake through the mackerel and add to the leeks with the creme fraiche and sweet chilli sauce.

Gently warm the sauce through, season, then add the drained pasta and toss through to coat.

COD IN LEMON BUTTER AND PARSLEY SAUCE

Poached fish is incredible – simple, light and melt-in-the-mouth – but it's even more incredible when it's poached in butter! Now, I'm not saying that this is the healthiest way to cook fish, but it is certainly one of the tastiest. The butter and lemon will separate a little in the pan as it cools; don't worry, this won't affect the taste. Basa fillets also work really well with this sauce.

 **FEEDS 4**

½ lemon
500g/1lb 2oz frozen cod fillets (or other white fish), defrosted
100g/4oz butter
Large handful of parsley, roughly chopped, plus extra to garnish
Freshly ground black pepper
Cooked rice, to serve

Cut the lemon into thin slices and arrange over the fish with some ground black pepper.

Melt the butter in a large frying pan, and add the fish and lemon. Cook on a low heat for 10 minutes, until cooked through and tender. Turn occasionally – be gentle so that the fish doesn't break. Add the parsley to the pan for the last 2 minutes of cooking.

Serve the cod fillets and lemon slices on a bed of rice. Spoon over some of the butter and garnish with some extra parsley.

COUSCOUS-COATED SALMON

This salmon makes a great dinner or lunch and is quick to prepare when you have unexpected guests. Spicy couscous is full of flavour and yet won't overpower the fish. Covering the salmon in couscous traps in the fish's juices and keeps it lovely and moist in the oven. This goes really well with boiled new potatoes and vegetables, or just a simple salad.

 FEEDS 4

1 packet of spicy couscous
165ml/5½fl oz boiling water
4 salmon fillets
3 tbsp plain flour
1 egg, beaten

Heat the oven to 200°C/400°F/Gas mark 6.

Put the couscous into a bowl and pour the boiling water over it. Cover the bowl with cling film and leave for 10 minutes.

Coat each of the salmon fillets in flour and then dip into the beaten egg.

Place the salmon in the bowl of couscous and gently press down, turn over and repeat, so that the salmon is coated.

Put all of the couscous-coated fillets onto a non-stick baking tray and bake in the oven for 15 minutes, until the couscous is crisp and golden and the salmon is cooked through.

4

VEGETARIAN

My brother has been a vegetarian since he was eight years old, so I grew up with a largely meat-free diet. I love vegetarian cooking; it requires you to be imaginative and creative and not simply rely on the flavours of the meat.

MOROCCAN CHICKPEA CURRY

I always have a tin of chickpeas in the cupboard, even if I have no immediate plans to cook with them. They are such a useful standby. They add texture, are high in fibre and, best of all, they're cheap! This dish is sweet and warming and has plenty of spice without being too hot.

 FEEDS 4

 FREEZABLE

400g/14oz tin of chickpeas
Olive oil, for frying
1 onion, finely sliced
½ butternut squash, peeled,
    deseeded and chopped
    into bite-sized chunks
2 garlic cloves, finely sliced
5cm/2in piece of fresh ginger,
    peeled and finely sliced
1 tsp ground cinnamon
2 tsp curry powder
    (see page 12)
25g/1oz sultanas
500g/1lb 2oz passata
50g/2oz spinach

Put the chickpeas in a saucepan with the liquid from the tin. Bring to the boil and simmer for 10 minutes. Drain and set them aside.

Heat some oil in a frying pan and add the onion and butternut squash. Fry on a low heat for 10 minutes. Add the garlic, ginger, cinnamon and curry powder to the pan and fry for a further 3 minutes, stirring occasionally.

Add the sultanas, chickpeas and passata to the pan and simmer on a low heat for 15 minutes, until the butternut squash and chickpeas are tender.

Add the spinach and simmer for a further 2 minutes before serving.

BUTTERNUT SQUASH RISOTTO

Technically this isn't actually a risotto because it's made with long grain rice rather than risotto rice. However, it tastes very risotto-like, as the rice still absorbs the flavours of the stock and the melted cheese gives it a creamy texture. Long grain rice cooks much quicker than risotto rice and doesn't need constant stirring like its high-maintenance cousin!

 FEEDS 4   ❄ **FREEZABLE**

300g/11oz long grain rice
2 vegetable stock cubes
650ml/23fl oz boiling water
½ butternut squash, peeled,
    deseeded and cut into
    bite-sized chunks
Olive oil, for roasting
    and frying
1 onion, very finely chopped
1 garlic clove, finely chopped
2 tsp dried sage
50g/2oz Parmesan cheese,
    plus extra for serving
200g/7oz roulé cheese

Heat the oven to 200°C/400°F/Gas mark 6.

Put the rice into a saucepan. Mix the stock cubes with the boiling water and stir until they have dissolved. Pour over the rice. Stir once, bring to the boil and simmer in a covered pan for 15 minutes, until the rice is cooked. If the rice is drying out too quickly, you can add a little more stock. Do not drain off the excess liquid.

Meanwhile, put the butternut squash in a roasting tin and drizzle with a little olive oil. Roast in the oven for 15 minutes.

In a separate large pan, fry the onion in olive oil on a low heat for 10 minutes.

Add the garlic and dried sage to the pan and fry for a further 5 minutes. Tip in the butternut squash with the Parmesan, roulé and rice (with any remaining stock from the pan) and stir well. Finish off with some extra grated Parmesan cheese.

QUORN MOUSSAKA

In my opinion, moussaka is the most satisfying way to use aubergines. This meal gets the best out of all of its components. If you are a vegetarian or are looking to add a veggie meal to your weekly dinners, this one's a must.

 **FEEDS 4**   ❄ **FREEZABLE**

1 onion, finely chopped
Olive oil, for frying
2 garlic cloves, finely chopped
1 tsp sugar
1 tsp ground cinnamon
1 tsp mixed herbs
500g/1lb 2oz passata
300g/11oz frozen
    Quorn mince
2 aubergines, cut into
    5cm/2in circles
Salt
2 medium potatoes, peeled
50g/2oz Cheddar
    cheese, grated

Fry the onion with some olive oil in a frying pan on a low heat for 10 minutes. Add the garlic, sugar, cinnamon and herbs and fry for a further 5 minutes.

Add the passata and frozen Quorn mince, stir through and take off the heat. Add a little water to the pan if it's too dry.

Sprinkle the aubergine slices with salt on both sides and leave them in a colander for 15 minutes to remove excess water. Rinse them in cold water and pat dry with kitchen paper.

Put the aubergine slices in a frying pan, a few at a time, drizzle with olive oil and gently fry for 2 minutes on each side.

Using the slicer side of a box grater, slice the potatoes into very thin discs. Put the potato slices in a pan of boiling salted water for 5 minutes until they are a little tender.

FOR THE CHEESE SAUCE
50g/2oz butter
50g/2oz plain flour
400ml/14fl oz milk
50g/2oz Cheddar
   cheese, grated

Heat the oven to 180°C/350°F/Gas mark 4.

Next make the sauce. Melt the butter in a saucepan, add the flour and mix thoroughly on a low heat until it's bubbling. Slowly add the milk, stirring constantly and bringing the mixture to the boil each time, before adding more milk. Keep stirring until it is smooth. Add the cheese and stir until it's melted.

Spoon a third of the Quorn mixture into an ovenproof baking dish and spread it out evenly. Add a layer of sliced potatoes, followed by a layer of aubergine. Add two more layers in this order: mince, potatoes and aubergine. Pour the cheese sauce over the top and sprinkle with the remaining cheese. Bake in the oven for 45 minutes until golden and bubbling.

RED PESTO, SUNDRIED TOMATO, FETA AND PISTACHIO SCONE-BASED PIZZA

This scone-based pizza is easy to make, as there is no kneading or proving required. This topping is a little lighter and healthier than the usual cheese and tomato, and the pistachio nuts provide protein and a lovely crunch! Although I have included this recipe in the vegetarian section, it can obviously be made with whatever toppings you like.

 FEEDS 4   ❄ **FREEZABLE**

FOR THE BASE
290g/10oz self-raising flour,
    plus extra for dusting
½ tsp salt
½ tsp baking powder
70g/3oz butter
150ml/5fl oz milk

FOR THE TOPPING
2 heaped tbsp red pesto
6 sundried tomatoes, sliced
100g/4oz feta, crumbled
Small handful of shelled
    pistachio nuts, crushed

Heat the oven to 200°C/400°F/Gas mark 6.

Add the flour, salt and baking powder to a large mixing bowl and combine. Rub in the butter so that it resembles fine breadcrumbs. Make a well in the centre of the mixture and add the milk. Press together to make dough.

Tip the dough onto a floured surface and roll it to the size and depth that you require. It will rise to approximately double the height in the oven. Transfer to a greased baking tray, then cook in the oven with no topping for 10 minutes.

Take the base out of the oven and spread it with the red pesto. Sprinkle over the sundried tomatoes and crumbled feta cheese and bake in the oven for a further 15 minutes.

Just before serving, sprinkle with the crushed pistachio nuts.

NOTE
For more pizza topping ideas please see page 41.

SUNDRIED TOMATO, SPINACH AND GOAT'S CHEESE SPAGHETTI

Sundried tomatoes go perfectly with the nutty flavours in goat's cheese... I could eat this all day long! Don't be put off by the small number of ingredients; this dish packs a huge amount of flavour.

 FEEDS 4

300g/11oz dried spaghetti
Bunch of spring onions,
    finely chopped
Olive oil, for frying
12 sundried tomatoes,
    roughly chopped
2 large handfuls of spinach
150g/5oz goat's cheese,
    roughly chopped
Salt and freshly ground
    black pepper

Cook the spaghetti in a pan of boiling water according to the pack instructions, until al dente. Drain.

Meanwhile, gently fry the spring onions in a pan with olive oil for 3 minutes.

Add the sundried tomatoes, spinach and cheese to the pan and cook on a low heat for a few seconds until the spinach has wilted and the cheese has started to melt.

Gently toss the drained spaghetti through the sauce until all of it is coated. Sprinkle with a little salt and a generous grind of black pepper.

SIMPLE VEGETABLE KORMA

This curry is great for the whole family. It has spice without being too hot for the kids and the sweet, creamy flavours make it a family favourite. If you want to make it healthier, use low-fat crème fraîche and light coconut milk.

 FEEDS 4

❄️ **FREEZABLE**

1 onion, finely sliced
Olive oil, for frying
1 garlic clove, finely chopped
10 Chantenay carrots, cut
    lengthways into three
10 cauliflower florets
10 broccoli florets
1 tsp chilli powder
1 tsp ground turmeric
½ tsp ground cumin
5cm/2in piece of fresh ginger,
    peeled and finely chopped
400ml/14fl oz tin of
    coconut milk
300g/11oz crème fraîche
200ml/7fl oz boiling water
    mixed with 1 vegetable
    stock cube
Rice or naan bread, to serve

Fry the onion in a pan with a little olive oil on a medium heat for 10 minutes, until soft. Add the garlic and gently fry for a further 5 minutes, then tip in the carrots, cauliflower and broccoli and fry for 5 minutes, moving them regularly around the pan.

Finally, add all of the spices and ginger and fry for a further 2 minutes.

Pour the coconut milk, crème fraîche and stock into a large mixing bowl. Using a hand blender, mix until smooth.

Pour the sauce into the pan over the veg, simmer uncovered for 15 minutes, until the vegetables are tender.

Serve with rice or naan bread.

VEGETARIAN TOAD IN THE HOLE

It took me years to get a decent rise on my Yorkshire pudding! It turns out, it was because I was using very cold milk, so make sure you warm the milk a little before using it and let the batter rest before cooking. Serve this with roast potatoes, veg and a big puddle of gravy!

 FEEDS 4

100g/4oz plain flour
½ tsp mixed herbs
Pinch of salt
1 egg
200ml/7fl oz warm milk
100ml/4fl oz warm water
2 tbsp olive oil
8 frozen Quorn, or
    other, sausages

Combine the flour, herbs and salt in a mixing bowl. Make a well in the middle and break the egg into it. Beat the egg, drawing in a little flour at a time until the mixture is a paste. Slowly add the warm milk and stir until all of the lumps have gone. Lightly whisk in the water. Set the batter aside for 1 hour.

Heat the oven to 220°C/425°F/Gas mark 7.

Put the olive oil and frozen sausages in a deep roasting tin, approximately 30 × 20cm/12 × 8in. Roll them around a little so that they are coated in the oil and put them in the oven. After 5 minutes the oil should be very hot and spitting a little. Remove from the oven and very quickly pour the batter around all of the sausages. Return to the oven and bake for 30–35 minutes, until risen and crispy.

HOMITY PIE

There is no better comfort food than a homity pie. This is my take on a childhood favourite. If you don't want to make one large pie, make individual pies by cutting out circles and placing them in a 12-hole muffin tray – they are perfect for a picnic.

FEEDS 4–6
OR MAKES
12 SMALL PIES

FREEZABLE

1 sheet of ready-rolled shortcrust pastry
800g/1¾lb potatoes, peeled and chopped into quarters
3 onions, sliced into semi-circles
Olive oil, for frying
2 garlic cloves, finely sliced
20g/1oz butter
25ml/1fl oz milk
2 tsp finely chopped fresh thyme
320g/11½oz grated Cheddar cheese
50g/2oz spinach

Heat the oven to 180°C/350°F/Gas mark 4. Grease a 25 × 20 × 7cm/10 × 8 × 2¾ deep pie dish.

Lay the pastry sheet in the pie dish and trim off the excess. Lay a sheet of baking parchment over the pastry, pour in some baking beans and bake blind for 25 minutes.

Put the potatoes in a large pan with cold salted water. Bring to the boil and simmer for 20 minutes, until the potatoes are tender and ready to mash.

Meanwhile, gently fry the onions in a pan with some olive oil for 15 minutes. For the last 5 minutes of frying, add the garlic.

Drain the potatoes and add the butter, milk and thyme. Mash the potatoes until they are smooth and fluffy. Add the onions and garlic, 250g/9oz of the grated cheese and the spinach, and mix well.

Put the filling into the baked pastry case and sprinkle the remaining grated cheese on the top. Bake in the oven for a further 20 minutes, until golden on top. Leave to cool a little before serving.

CAULIFLOWER CHEESE WITH A KICK

Classic cauliflower cheese was the first meal I ever learnt to cook. The addition of digestive biscuits to the topping for this version adds a lovely sweetness to the dish. You haven't tried cauliflower cheese until you've tried this! If you want to make it a little healthier, just reduce the amount of grated cheese you use.

 **FEEDS 4**   ❄ **FREEZABLE**

1 cauliflower, broken into
    florets, discarding
    large stalks
60g/2½oz butter
60g/2½oz plain flour
1 tsp chilli powder
500ml/18fl oz milk
230g/8oz Cheddar
    cheese, grated
1 tsp English mustard
2 digestive biscuits

Heat the oven to 200°C/400°F/Gas mark 6.

Put the cauliflower florets in a saucepan and cover with cold salted water. Bring to the boil, then simmer for 15 minutes.

In a separate saucepan, melt the butter. When melted, add the flour and chilli powder, stirring continuously until it is a bubbling paste. Gradually add the milk, stirring continuously and bringing it to the boil each time, before adding more milk. Once you have used all of the milk and there are no lumps in the sauce, remove the pan from the heat. Add 130g/4½oz of the cheese and the mustard and stir until the cheese has melted.

Drain the cauliflower and place in a baking dish. Pour the cheese sauce evenly over the top.

Put the digestives in a food processor and whizz to a crumb. Mix with the remaining cheese and sprinkle over the cauliflower cheese, then bake in the oven for 30 minutes, until the cheese is golden and crispy.

VEGETARIAN MEATLOAF

This looks and tastes a lot like meatloaf but it uses Quorn mince as a meat substitute. It holds its form and slices really well, making it a great vegetarian alternative for a roast dinner. I usually serve it with roast potatoes, veg and gravy for a midweek mini-roast!

 FEEDS 4

Olive oil, for frying
   and greasing
1 onion, finely sliced
1 garlic clove, finely sliced
1 celery stalk, finely sliced
1 carrot, grated
300g/11oz frozen
   Quorn mince
2 tsp mixed herbs
1 vegetable stock cube,
   crumbled
1 tsp Marmite
1 egg, beaten
2 slices of bread, whizzed
   into crumbs

Heat the oven to 200°C/400°F/Gas mark 6. Grease a 900g/2lb loaf tin.

Heat a little olive oil in a large pan and fry the onion, garlic, celery and grated carrot for 15 minutes, until soft and translucent.

Add the frozen Quorn mince, herbs, stock cube, Marmite and 1 tablespoon of water to the pan and fry for 5 minutes. Stir regularly to prevent it from sticking to the bottom. Transfer the mixture to a large bowl and add the beaten egg and the breadcrumbs. Stir until the bread has absorbed a lot of the moisture.

Spoon the mixture into the loaf tin and press the mince down firmly with the back of the spoon, especially around the edges. Bake in the oven for 40 minutes.

Leave to cool a little before removing from the tin and slicing.

QUORN CASSEROLE

This is a perfect midweek meal. High in protein, low in fat and with some left over for lunch the next day. I use squash, parsnip and carrots as the main vegetables, but you could use any veg that needs using up.

 FEEDS 4

1 onion, finely sliced
Olive oil, for frying
½ butternut squash, peeled and
    chopped into even chunks
2 carrots, peeled and chopped
    into even chunks
2 parsnips, peeled and
    chopped into even chunks
    (slightly larger than the
    carrots and squash)
1 garlic clove, finely chopped
2 tbsp flour
300g/11oz Quorn
    frozen pieces
2 tsp mixed herbs
2 vegetable stock cubes
1 litre/1¾ pints boiling water
Handful of frozen peas

Fry the onion in a pan on a low heat with some olive oil for 10 minutes.

Add the squash, carrots, parsnips and garlic to the onions. Add a little more olive oil and fry on a low heat, stirring regularly, for 5 minutes.

Add the flour, frozen Quorn and dried herbs to the pan and cook for a further 2 minutes, stirring to ensure it doesn't stick to the bottom.

Dissolve the stock cubes into the boiling water. Slowly add the stock to the vegetables, stirring all the time to allow the sauce to thicken. Add the peas and simmer on a low heat for 20 minutes, until the vegetables are tender.

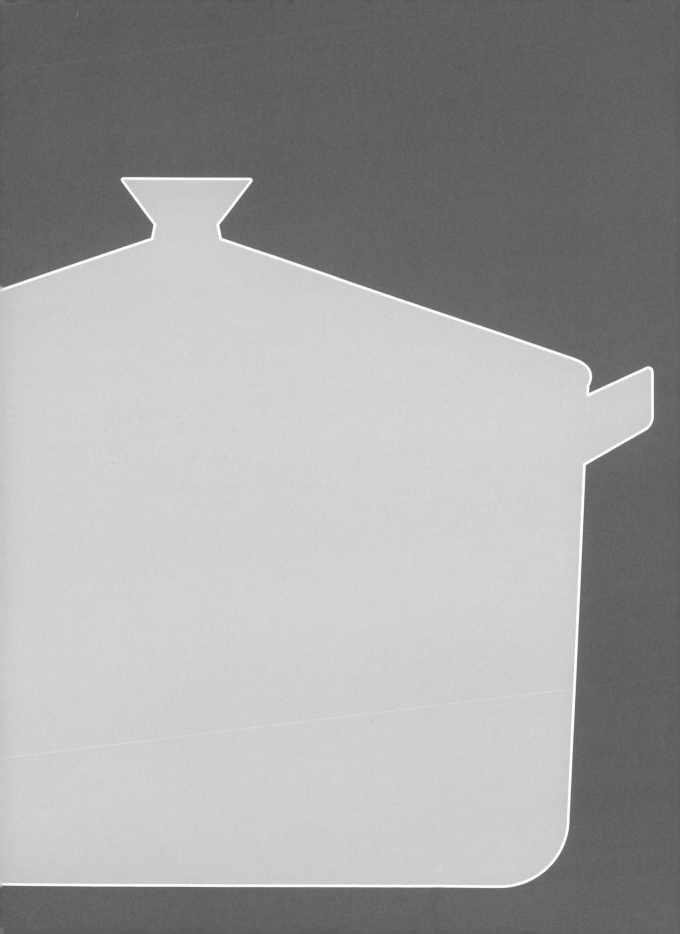

5

CHICKEN

This is my favourite chapter in the book. These are the meals that I cook most regularly, and all are hearty plate-fillers. I nearly always buy bags of frozen chicken and defrost it as I need it. It's a really economical way to buy food, as nothing gets wasted.

CHICKEN, POTATO AND CHORIZO TRAYBAKE

Ahhh, the traybake! Just 10 minutes of hands-on time, an hour in the oven and then you have an all-in-one meal! Perfect after a busy day. This recipe is packed with flavour and the chicken literally falls off the bone. If you like it spicy, add a finely chopped chilli.

 **FEEDS 4**

500g/1lb 2oz baby Maris Peer potatoes, evenly chopped
1 mixed bag of 3 peppers, deseeded and each cut into about 16 chunks
300g/11oz bag of shallots, peeled and cut in half
200g/7oz chorizo ring
1 tsp paprika
½ tsp chilli powder
1 tbsp olive oil
8 chicken thighs
Crusty bread, to serve

Heat the oven to 200°C/400°F/Gas mark 6.

Place the potatoes around the edge of a large roasting tray and scatter the peppers chunks evenly within them. Mix the shallots with the peppers.

Remove the ends of the chorizo, cut the ring into thick slices, roughly the width of two £1 coins, and add to the tray.

In a cup, mix the paprika, chilli and olive oil. Pour half the mixture over the vegetables. Use your hands to ensure they are all coated in the oil and move the potatoes back to the edges of the tray.

Place the chicken thighs on top of the peppers, chorizo and onion, skin side up. Drizzle the remaining oil over the chicken. Cook in the oven for 1 hour, or until the chicken is cooked through. Drain any excess oil from the chorizo from the tray before serving with crusty bread.

CHICKEN, CHEESE AND LEEK PATTIES

These patties are perfect for picnics or packed lunches as they taste great hot or cold. This recipe makes a little more filling than you need, so try heating up what you have left and serving it with mashed potato. If you don't want to use Gorgonzola you can use all Cheddar.

 **FEEDS 6**   ❄ **FREEZABLE**

2 chicken breast fillets, cut
    into 1cm/½in cubes
1 leek, chopped in half
    and finely sliced
Olive oil, for frying
1 tsp plain flour
100ml/4fl oz milk
50g/2oz Gorgonzola, cubed
50g/2oz Cheddar
    cheese, cubed
1 tsp finely chopped parsley
1 sheet of ready-rolled
    puff pastry
1 egg, beaten

Heat the oven to 220°C/425°F/Gas mark 7. Lightly grease a baking tray.

Fry the chicken and leek in a little olive oil on a low heat for 10 minutes. Add the flour and stir continuously on a low heat for a further 2 minutes.

Gradually add the milk to the chicken and leek, stirring all the time. When all the milk is used and the sauce is smooth and thick, simmer for 2 minutes. Add the Gorgonzola, Cheddar and parsley and stir in until the cheese has melted. Leave to cool a little.

Using a pastry cutter or large mug, cut out 12 circles from the pastry and transfer to the baking tray. Put 2 teaspoons of the filling in the centre of each pastry circle, then, using a pastry brush, go around the outside edge of the circle with beaten egg. Place a second circle on top and, using a fork, press around the sides to join the pastry together.

Make the remaining patties, glaze with beaten egg and bake in the oven for 30 minutes.

SAUCY CHICKEN AND PEPPER PIE

I used to make a 'deconstructed' version of this dish, which consisted of chicken and chorizo casserole served with mashed potato. One day it occurred to me that I could just turn this into a one-pot meal. Serve this with salad and garlic bread; it is a really filling dinner that goes a long way.

 FEEDS 6 PLUS LEFTOVERS

❄ **FREEZABLE**

800g/1¾lb potatoes, peeled and cut into quarters
1 tbsp milk
25g/1oz butter
2 onions, finely sliced
Olive oil, for frying
4 chicken breast fillets, cut into strips
2 garlic cloves, finely sliced
2 red peppers, deseeded and finely sliced
170g/6oz chorizo sausage, sliced
1 tsp paprika
1 tsp chilli powder
500g/1lb 2oz passata
50g/2oz Cheddar cheese, grated
Salt and freshly ground black pepper

Put the potatoes in a large saucepan and cover them in cold, salted water. Bring to the boil and simmer for 20 minutes, or until the potatoes are tender.

Drain the potatoes, mash with the milk and butter until smooth, then season with salt and pepper.

Heat the oven to 200°C/400°F/Gas mark 6.

Fry the onions in olive oil for 10 minutes on a low heat, stirring occasionally, then add the chicken with the garlic and fry for 5 minutes on a low heat, until sealed and lightly browned. Add the red peppers, chorizo, paprika and chilli and fry for a further 5 minutes.

Add the passata to the pan and simmer for 10 minutes, before pouring the mixture into an ovenproof dish.

Spread the mashed potato evenly over the chicken and chorizo filling and gently press down. Sprinkle over the grated Cheddar cheese and bake in the oven for 50 minutes.

SPICY BREADED CHICKEN

This is a great healthy alternative to processed oven-baked chicken, and it's almost as quick to cook! I always serve these with potato wedges and a big dollop of mayonnaise. There is no doubt that these fillets have a bit of a kick to them, but not so much that my children won't eat them. If you fancy something with a little more fire, add an extra ½ teaspoon of chilli powder.

MAKES 9

FREEZABLE

Olive oil, for greasing
2 slices of bread (I use granary)
½ tsp salt
1 tsp freshly ground black pepper
1 tsp ground cumin
1 tsp chilli powder
1 tsp paprika
25g/1oz plain flour
1 egg, beaten
375g/13oz chicken breast mini fillets (approximately 9)

Heat the oven to 200°C/400°F/Gas mark 6. Grease a baking tray.

Put the bread, salt, pepper, cumin, chilli powder and paprika into a food processor and whizz to breadcrumbs. Place the breadcrumbs in a bowl.

Put the flour in a separate bowl and the beaten egg in another. Make sure the chicken fillets are roughly the same thickness. Cut any thick breasts in half lengthways, so that they all take the same time to cook.

Dip each fillet first into the flour and then into the egg, then put the fillet into the spicy breadcrumbs and press down on both sides to make sure that it is coated all over. Repeat this for all the fillets. Place on the greased baking tray and bake in the oven for 20 minutes, or until the chicken is cooked through.

CORIANDER, CHILLI AND LIME CHICKEN

I love a barbecue! It's really nice to have a selection of marinated meats and different salads to serve up on a summer's day. This marinade is full of flavour and really quick to make. Don't be scared off by the whole chilli as some of the heat is lost in the cooking. I always cook this on the barbecue, but you can cook it on a griddle if the weather is against you! Serve with coleslaw or any of your favourite barbecue accompaniments.

MAKES 9 MINI FILLETS

FREEZABLE

Large handful of coriander
    leaves
1 red chilli, deseeded
    and finely chopped
1 garlic clove, thinly sliced
Juice of 1 lime, zest of ½
9 chicken mini fillets

Add the coriander, chilli, garlic, lime juice and zest to a food processor and pulse until combined and an even consistency.

Put the raw chicken into a bowl and pour the marinade over it. Cover it in cling film and refrigerate for 30 minutes.

Arrange the marinated chicken onto the barbecue and cook for 10–15 minutes, turning regularly, until the chicken is cooked through and no longer pink.

CHICKEN CAESAR SALAD

You can't beat a Caesar salad – it's quick to prepare and filling. You can obviously buy a ready-made Caesar sauce, but sometimes it's nice to make your own. If you are looking to make this meal a little healthier, just replace the mayonnaise with light mayonnaise.

 FEEDS 4

2 slices of bread
Olive oil, to drizzle
2 Little Gem lettuces
4 radishes
150g/5oz roast chicken
    breast slices
Shavings of Parmesan or
    Cheddar cheese, to serve

FOR THE SAUCE
3 tbsp mayonnaise
1 garlic clove, finely chopped
5 anchovies, finely chopped,
    with 2 tsp oil reserved
    from the jar or tin
Juice of ½ lemon
½ tsp freshly ground
    black pepper

Heat the oven to 200°C/400°F/Gas mark 6.

To make the croutons; tear the slices of bread into bite-sized pieces and drizzle with olive oil. Place them on a baking tray and cook in the oven for 10 minutes until crisp.

To make the sauce, put all the ingredients in a bowl and stir well until combined.

Slice the lettuces widthways to make discs and divide among 4 plates.

Using the slicer side of a cheese grater, thinly slice the radishes and arrange on the plates.

Divide the roast chicken and the croutons among the plates then drizzle a generous portion of sauce over each salad and finish with shavings of Parmesan or Cheddar cheese and a good grind of pepper.

THAI CHICKEN NOODLE BROTH

I love cooking this meal. The smell of garlic, ginger and spring onions mixed with the spices is amazing and packs so much flavour into what is quite an innocent-looking dish. When you have eaten the noodles and chicken I guarantee you will be drinking the broth from the bowl – it is definitely too good to waste!

 FEEDS 4

❄ **FREEZABLE**

Bunch of spring onions, finely chopped
1 red chilli, deseeded and finely chopped
1 garlic clove, finely chopped
3cm/1¼in piece of fresh ginger, peeled and finely sliced
Olive oil, for frying
3 chicken breast fillets, cut into slices
1 tsp chilli powder
1 tsp ground cumin
1 chicken stock cube
450ml/¾ pint boiling water
180g/6oz medium dried noodles (roughly 3 nests)
100g/4oz mangetout
Salt and freshly ground black pepper

Add the spring onions, chilli, garlic and ginger to a large pan, drizzle with olive oil and fry on a low heat for 3 minutes, stirring regularly so that they do not burn.

Put the chicken in the pan and fry for a further 5 minutes, until it is lightly browned. Add salt and pepper, chilli powder and cumin to the pan and fry for 2 minutes, stirring regularly.

Dissolve the chicken stock cube in the boiling water, then add the stock, noodles and mangetout to the pan. Cover and simmer for 10 minutes, until the chicken is cooked through and the noodles are tender.

CASHEW CHICKEN STIR-FRY

Once you have made this recipe, I feel fairly confident it will become one of your regular meals. It ticks all of the boxes: it's quick to make, healthy and ridiculously tasty! If whole cashew nuts are a bit much for you, crush them a little with a rolling pin after frying them.

 FEEDS 4

Olive oil, for frying
110g/4oz unsalted
     cashew nuts
4 chicken breast fillets, sliced
     into bite-sized pieces
300g/11oz spring greens,
     sliced into ribbons
2 garlic cloves, sliced
Bunch of spring onions, cut
     into 3cm/1¼in widths
3cm/1¼in piece of fresh
     ginger, peeled and
     sliced into matchsticks
2 red chillies, deseeded
     and roughly chopped
2 tbsp soy sauce

Drizzle a little olive oil in a wok and heat it for 1 minute until spitting a little. Add the cashew nuts to the wok and gently fry for 1 minute until browned – keep the nuts moving so that they don't burn. Remove the cashew nuts and place on some kitchen paper to absorb the excess oil.

Place the chicken in the wok and gently fry for 5 minutes, until the chicken is no longer pink. Add the spring greens, garlic, spring onions, ginger and red chillies to the wok. Pour in the soy sauce and fry on a medium heat, turning regularly, for 10 minutes, or until the chicken is cooked through.

Add the cashews to the wok for the last minute of cooking and serve.

FIERY PEANUT AND HONEY CHICKEN NOODLE SALAD

I buy bags of frozen chicken whenever available, and I often find that I have a couple of chicken breasts extra. This salad can be put together in 10 minutes and, unlike other more leafy salads, this one is really filling. We usually have this as a dinner, but it works really well as a packed lunch. Just pop it in a container and keep the dressing in a separate pot to pour on just before you eat it.

 FEEDS 4

2 nests of medium
   dried noodles
2 carrots
4 spring green leaves
4 cold cooked chicken
   breasts or equivalent
   leftover chicken
Salt and freshly ground
   black pepper

FOR THE DRESSING
4 tsp smooth peanut butter
4 tsp honey
4 tsp soy sauce
2 tsp olive oil
2 tsp cold water
4 spring onions, very
   finely chopped
1–2 red chillies, deseeded
   and finely chopped, plus
   extra slices to serve

Put the noodles into a saucepan, cover with boiling water and simmer for 4 minutes with the lid on. Drain the noodles and immediately immerse them in cold water. Leave them in the water for a few minutes until they are cooled right through, then drain. This will prevent them from overcooking and sticking together.

Chop the ends off the carrots and peel them. Discard the skin and continue to peel, creating ribbons, using as much of the carrot as you can. Add to the noodles.

Put the spring greens leaves together, fold them in half lengthways and then in half again. Slicing widthways, cut the greens into thin ribbons. Add the greens to the noodles.

To make the dressing, combine all the ingredients together in a bowl. Pour the dressing over the noodles and, using your hands, combine all of the ingredients, making sure they are all coated in the dressing.

Divide the noodles between 4 bowls, then slice or tear the chicken over the noodles. Season with salt and pepper and garnish with a few slices of red chilli.

HAI GREEN CURRY

There are literally hundreds of Thai green curry recipes out there. Some are complex and call for kaffir lime leaves, others use a ready-made curry paste. This recipe falls somewhere in between. It's made from scratch, but it is an all-in-one method with fewer ingredients. If you like your curry a little milder just use one chilli.

 FEEDS 4

❄ **FREEZABLE**

2 garlic cloves, sliced
1 tbsp brown sugar
Handful of fresh coriander,
    plus extra to serve
2 red chillies, deseeded
    and sliced
3cm/1¼in piece of fresh
    ginger, peeled and sliced
Grated zest of 1 lime
750g/1lb 11oz chicken
    breast fillets, sliced
Olive oil, for frying
400ml/14fl oz coconut milk
100g/4oz green beans,
    ends trimmed
135g/4½oz baby corn
Cooked rice, to serve

Put the garlic, sugar, coriander, chillies, ginger and lime zest into a food processor and blend to a paste.

Fry the chicken in olive oil on a low heat for 8 minutes, until slightly browned. Add the curry paste to the chicken and fry for a further 2 minutes, stirring regularly.

Add the coconut milk, green beans and baby corn and stir well. Simmer on a low heat for 15 minutes, or until the chicken is cooked through.

Serve with rice and some roughly chopped coriander.

SATURDAY NIGHT CHICKEN BALTI

Although this recipe has quite a long list of ingredients, they are mostly things you will have in your cupboards, and it is a really quick, flavoursome curry. It's medium in heat, so if you like it hotter or milder, vary the amount of chilli powder you use. Serve it with rice or naan bread.

FEEDS 4

FREEZABLE

1 onion, chopped
2 red peppers, deseeded
    and sliced
Olive oil, for frying
4 chicken breasts, cut into
    3cm/1¼in pieces
2 tbsp tomato purée
1 garlic clove, finely chopped
5cm/2in piece of fresh ginger,
    peeled and finely chopped
Juice of ½ lime
1 tsp ground coriander
1 tsp ground cumin
1 tsp chilli powder
½ tsp ground cinnamon
1 tsp sugar
1 tsp mango chutney
400g/14oz tin chopped
    tomatoes
Handful of fresh coriander,
    chopped, to garnish
    (optional)

Fry the onion and peppers in a pan with some olive oil on a low heat for 10 minutes. Add the chicken to the pan and fry for a further 5 minutes, until the chicken is cooked through and no longer pink.

In a small bowl, combine the tomato purée, garlic, ginger, lime juice, ground spices, sugar and mango chutney.

Pour this mixture over the chicken and peppers and stir until they are evenly coated. Fry on a low heat for a further 5 minutes, stirring occasionally so that it doesn't stick to the bottom of the pan. Stir in the tomatoes and simmer on a low heat for 20 minutes, until the chicken is cooked through.

Serve with chopped coriander and a side of rice, if you like.

6

BEEF AND PORK

In some ways, this chapter is the main event. The recipes in this section are all hearty main meals – many of which are perfect if you're cooking for lots of people. If you only try one recipe, give the Pork, Mustard and Cider Stew a go – it's like a great big hug on a plate!

SAUSAGE AND ROASTED VEGETABLE PILAF

I have been making this for years. My husband has given it the name 'Sausage Surprise', as I change the ingredients based on what's in the cupboard! Sometimes it works, sometimes it doesn't – I will say that swede won't be repeated! This version is my favourite combination of vegetables and spices, but you can make this dish your own.

 FEEDS 4

❄ **FREEZABLE**

1 red and 1 yellow pepper, deseeded and chopped into equal-sized pieces
2 onions, sliced into wedges
1 courgette, evenly sliced
1/3 butternut squash, peeled and cut into chunks
2 garlic cloves
12 pork sausages
Olive oil, for drizzling
2 packets of microwave basmati rice
½ tsp ground cumin
2 tsp paprika
Salt and freshly ground black pepper

Heat the oven to 190°C/375°F/Gas mark 5.

Place the peppers, onions and courgette into a roasting tin with the butternut squash. Give the peeled garlic cloves a quick bash with the end of a rolling pin and add to the tin.

Arrange the sausages around the vegetables and drizzle generously with olive oil. Use your hands to ensure all of the vegetables and sausages are coated and then put the roasting tin in the oven for 30 minutes.

About 10 minutes before the sausages and vegetables are cooked, remove them from the oven. Add the rice, cumin, paprika, salt and pepper and little more olive oil.

Make sure everything is combined then return to the oven for the final 10 minutes. Give it a stir before serving.

BOSTON BEANS

This is my take on this famous American dish. I substitute the traditionally used black treacle for maple syrup; doing this means you don't need to add additional sugar as maple syrup is much sweeter. Most recipes call for dried haricot beans and passata, but that makes what should be a simple dish a bit of a faff, so I use tins of baked beans instead.

 FEEDS 4

Olive oil, for frying
1 onion, finely sliced
150g/5oz bacon lardons
2 garlic cloves, finely sliced
2 tsp paprika
1 tsp Dijon mustard
1 tbsp maple syrup
2 × 400g/14oz tins of
  baked beans
Freshly ground black pepper
Hot buttered toast or crusty
  bread to serve

Heat a little oil in a large frying pan, and gently fry the onion and bacon lardons on a low heat for 10 minutes.

Add the garlic to the pan with the paprika, a grinding of black pepper, the mustard and syrup. Fry for a further 3 minutes, stirring intermittently to prevent it from sticking to the pan. Then add the baked beans to the pan and gently heat through; season with salt.

Serve on its own or with hot buttered toast or crusty bread.

PORK LOIN STEAKS AND SAGE MOZZARELLA SAUCE

I first made this sauce to go with butternut squash pasta. It's so moreish, I had to come up with other dishes to go with it! Pork and sage are a great combination and the mozzarella balances any bitterness. I always serve this with a generous helping of mashed potato.

 FEEDS 4

Olive oil, for frying
4 pork loin steaks
50g/2oz butter
1 tsp dried sage
1 ball of mozzarella
1 tbsp milk
Salt and freshly ground
　　black pepper

Heat the oven to 200°C/400°F/Gas mark 6.

In a hot frying pan, heat a tablespoon of olive oil. Add the pork steaks to the pan and fry for 1 minute on each side on a high heat.

In the meantime, put a roasting tray in the oven for 3 minutes until it's hot.

Put the steaks in the roasting tray along with the juices from the pan and cook in the oven for approximately 5 minutes. They may need a little more or less time depending on their thickness. Remove from the oven and leave the steaks to rest for 10 minutes.

Melt the butter in a saucepan and add the dried sage. Let the butter simmer with the sage for 2 minutes on a low heat. Tear up the mozzarella and add to the butter in the pan, then pour in the milk and season with salt and pepper. Using a hand blender, whizz the ingredients to a smooth sauce, then heat through without boiling and drizzle over the pork. Serve with your choice of vegetable.

Any leftover sauce can be stored in the fridge for up to 3 days for a pasta or dipping sauce.

GORGONZOLA BURGER

As far as burgers are concerned, my husband is very hard to please. Burgers are his first choice whenever we eat out, so it's fair to say he is a bit of an expert! He has declared this to be one of the best burgers he's eaten! Give it a go! It's satisfying to cook and really is very tasty.

 MAKES 4 LARGE BURGERS

❄️ **FREEZABLE**

Olive oil, for frying
1 onion, finely sliced
1 garlic clove, finely sliced
500g/1lb 2oz Aberdeen
    Angus beef mince
1 egg, beaten
1 tsp Dijon mustard
1 tsp roughly chopped
    thyme leaves
100g/4oz Gorgonzola,
    roughly cut into cubes
Flour, for dusting
Salt and freshly ground
    black pepper
4 burger buns (I like brioche
    buns if I can get them)
Lettuce, tomato and
    mayonnaise, to serve

Heat the olive oil in a pan on a low heat and fry the onion for 5 minutes. Add the garlic to the pan and fry for a further 5 minutes.

Put the beef mince into a mixing bowl and tip in the fried onions and garlic, beaten egg, mustard, thyme leaves and salt and pepper to taste.

Add the Gorgonzola cubes to the beef and, using your hands, combine all of the ingredients – make sure they are evenly distributed by pressing them firmly through the mince. Divide the mixture into 4 and roll each one into a ball. Put each ball on a lightly floured surface and press down firmly into a burger shape. Press around the edges to ensure that they are the same thickness all the way through. Cover the burgers and refrigerate for at least 30 minutes.

Heat a little oil in a frying pan and fry the burgers for 5 minutes on each side, or until the fat is running clear and the burgers are cooked through. Leave to rest before serving on a brioche burger bun with lettuce, tomato and mayonnaise.

SMOKY SAUSAGE AND BACON PASTA

I discovered this recipe on a camping trip last year. I needed to feed two families with a meal that could be cooked on a double camping stove. Everyone loved it and it's become a bit of a regular for us. This two-pan wonder is comfort food at its best. If you want to make it a little healthier, swap the soured cream for light crème fraîche.

FEEDS 6

350g/12oz conchiglie
    (shell) pasta
8 pork sausages
Drizzle of olive oil
1 onion, finely sliced
1 red pepper, deseeded
    and finely sliced
6 rashers of smoked bacon,
    cut into thick strips
2 tsp paprika
½ tsp chilli powder
300ml/10fl oz soured cream
2 tbsp passata
Salt and freshly ground
    black pepper

Place the pasta in a large saucepan of boiling salted water and simmer for 10–15 minutes, until al dente.

Place the sausages in a large, non-stick frying pan and drizzle over a little olive oil. Fry for 5 minutes on a medium heat, turning regularly. Remove the sausages from the pan and slice each one into 6 or 7 pieces, before returning to the pan.

Add the onion, red pepper and bacon to the sausages and fry for a further 10 minutes, until the sausage and bacon are cooked through and the onions and peppers are soft. Stir in the paprika and chilli powder and fry for a further 3 minutes. Add the soured cream and passata to the pan and simmer until the sauce has heated through.

Drain the pasta and add to the sauce, mixing well before seasoning with ground black pepper and serving.

SAUSAGE MEATBALL MARINARA SUB

I really wanted to include this dish in the book. Firstly, it's a really versatile recipe: you can serve the meatballs with spaghetti or mashed potato, instead of in a sub, and the marinara sauce is great for pasta and pizza – even without the meatballs. Secondly, it's absolutely delicious and a weekend favourite in our house!

 **MAKES 4 SUBS**   **FREEZABLE**

6 Cumberland sausages
1 slice of bread
1 tsp dried oregano
2 tbsp plain flour
Olive oil, for frying
4 rolls – I like using sub
    rolls if I can get them
Grated cheese, to serve

FOR THE MARINARA SAUCE
Olive oil, for frying
1 onion, finely chopped
1 garlic clove, finely chopped
1 tsp dried oregano
½ tsp dried sage
½ tsp dried thyme
1 tsp sugar
1 tsp balsamic vinegar
500g/1lb 2oz passata
Salt and freshly ground
    black pepper

Run a knife lengthways down each sausage skin. Open up the skin and scoop the sausage meat into a mixing bowl.

Blitz the slice of bread in a food processor, until it becomes fine breadcrumbs. Add the breadcrumbs and the oregano to the sausage meat and use your hands to mix it all together.

Sprinkle the flour onto a clean worktop. Divide the sausage mince into 16, and roll each one between the palms of your hands until you have a neat meatball. Gently roll them in the flour to prevent them from sticking to the pan.

Heat a drizzle of olive oil in a large, non-stick frying pan and fry the meatballs on a medium heat for 15 minutes, moving them regularly so that they are browned all over.

In the meantime, make the sauce. Place the chopped onion in a pan with a drizzle of olive oil and gently fry for 10 minutes, until soft and translucent. Add the garlic, dried herbs, sugar and balsamic vinegar and fry for a further 5 minutes, stirring regularly.

Add the passata, seasoning and the meatballs and simmer for a further 10 minutes covered, until the meatballs are warmed through. Serve the meatballs and sauce on a roll and finish off with a little cheese.

CHILLI BEEF CANNELLONI

This recipe substitutes lasagne sheets with tortilla wraps. They are the same consistency as lasagne when baked, but are much less fiddly to cook with. This is a great dish for when you have friends over; it goes a long way, can be cooked ahead of time and only needs a salad to accompany it.

 FEEDS 6

❄ **FREEZABLE**

5 tortilla wraps
Olive oil, for frying
200g/7oz tub of soft cheese
1 red chilli, deseeded
    and finely chopped
3 tsp chilli powder
2 tsp ground cumin
150g/5oz Cheddar
    cheese, grated
1 onion, finely sliced
500g/1lb 2oz beef mince
1 garlic clove, finely sliced
1 tsp sugar
400g/14oz tin of kidney
    beans, drained
500g1lb 2oz passata

Preheat the oven to 200°C/400°F/Gas mark 6.

Gently fry the tortillas one at a time in a little olive oil for a minute on each side. Set aside.

Put the soft cheese in a mixing bowl with the chopped chilli, 1 teaspoon of the chilli powder, 1 teaspoon of the ground cumin and 50g/2oz of the cheese. Divide the mixture between the tortillas and spread it evenly over one side, making sure you go right to the edges. Fold each tortilla in half, then place them in a row, slightly overlapping, along the bottom of a baking dish.

Fry the onion in a little olive oil in a pan on a low heat for 5 minutes. Add the beef mince and garlic and fry for a further 5 minutes, stirring occasionally. Add the remaining chilli powder and ground cumin and the sugar and fry for a further 2 minutes. Finally, add the kidney beans and passata and simmer on a low heat for 10 minutes.

Pour the contents of the pan over the tortillas in the baking dish. Sprinkle the remaining cheese over the top and bake for 25 minutes, until the cheese is golden brown. Leave to cool a little before cutting into slices and serving.

STEAK AND POTATO SALAD WITH CREAMY HORSERADISH DRESSING

Let's be clear, this is not a Tuesday night 'I'm going to be good' kind of salad. This is a Saturday night in front of the telly kind of salad! It's tasty and very filling; the fact that it's healthy is purely incidental!

 FEEDS 2

2 × sirloin steaks (30-day
    matured if you can get it)
50g/2oz butter
½ × 120g/4½oz bag of pea
    shoots and baby leaves,
    or other leafy salad
360g/12oz pack of baby
    potatoes with herb butter
Olive oil, for frying
3 radishes, finely sliced
Salt and freshly ground
    black pepper

FOR THE DRESSING
2 heaped tbsp soured cream
2 tsp horseradish sauce
½ tsp lemon juice

Using your hands, rub both sides of the steak with the butter. This will be clumpy in places. Then give each steak a generous sprinkling of salt and black pepper and set aside.

Divide the pea shoots and baby leaves between two plates.

Put the herb potatoes into the microwave and cook according to the packet instructions. When the potatoes are cooked, add to the salad leaves.

Meanwhile, add a drizzle of olive oil to a griddle or frying pan and turn the heat up. Leave the oil for a couple of minutes, until it's smoking hot. Put the steaks in the pan and cook for 3 minutes on the first side, then turn over and cook for a further 2 minutes. Remove the steaks from the pan and put them on a wire rack to rest – this will allow some of the fat to drain out.

When the steaks have rested for 5 minutes, slice them into manageable pieces and place on the salad. Arrange the radish slices on the plates.

Mix all of the dressing ingredients together, season, then pour liberally over the salad.

THE BEST STEAK DINNER EVER!

A friend of ours, who is an amazing cook, first introduced us to a variation of this recipe – and we loved it! Thirty-day matured steaks are a dream to cook with and are unbelievably tender. I'm not going to pretend that this is the cheapest meal in the world, but it's worth it for a special occasion, and the steaks you can buy from discount supermarkets are a lot less expensive than those from a traditional supermarket, without compromising on quality – I promise!

 FEEDS 4

4 × 30-day matured ribeye
steaks (remove from
the fridge 30 minutes
before cooking)
100g/4oz butter
4 large baked potatoes
Olive oil, for frying
12 frozen onion rings
200g/7oz Gorgonzola
200g/7oz asparagus tips
Salt and freshly ground
black pepper

Heat the oven to 200°C/400°F/Gas mark 6.

Using your hands, rub both sides of the steak with half of the butter. This will be clumpy in places. Then give each steak a generous sprinkling of salt and black pepper and set aside.

Wash and dry the potatoes and, using a sharp knife, pierce several holes in them, right to the centre on both sides. Put the potatoes in the microwave on full power (two at a time) for 5 minutes on each side. Place the potatoes on a baking tray and, using a pastry brush, brush them with olive oil. Cook the potatoes in the oven for 15 minutes.

Remove the potatoes from the oven and put the onions rings in to bake on a roasting tray. Cut each potato down the middle, making sure both halves are still attached. Using a fork, gently mash the potato inside the skin, to allow the butter and cheese to melt all the way through. Divide the remaining butter between each of the potatoes and use a fork to press it into the potato flesh.

(continued)

Divide the Gorgonzola into 4 pieces and put one inside each of the potatoes, gently pushing each half back together to keep the cheese inside. Return the potatoes to the oven for a further 10 minutes.

Meanwhile, put a drizzle of olive oil in a griddle or frying pan and turn the heat up. Leave the oil for a couple of minutes, until it is smoking hot. Put the steaks in the pan, two at a time, and cook for 3 minutes on the first side, then turn over and cook for a further 2 minutes. Remove from the pan to a wire rack to rest and allow some of the fat to drain out, then repeat with the remaining steaks.

Using the same griddle you cooked the steaks in, fry the asparagus tips, drizzled with olive oil, salt and pepper, on a medium-high heat, for 5–7 minutes, moving them around occasionally, until they are tender.

Divide the asparagus between 4 plates. Add a steak, a potato and some onion rings and serve immediately.

NOTE
You can serve with just half a baked potato each if you have a smaller appetite or are cooking for children.

PORK, MUSTARD AND CIDER STEW

I love this recipe. It's the sort of meal that makes you look forward to winter. It's so simple to make and is full of the heartwarming, salty deliciousness that every stew should have! It's best served on a big pile of mashed potato, but goes well with rice too.

 FEEDS 4 ❄ **FREEZABLE**

25g/1oz butter
300g/11oz pork medallions,
    cut into bite-sized pieces
200g/7oz smoked bacon,
    cut into thick strips
2 onions, each cut into
    12 wedges
1 tsp dried sage
2 tbsp plain flour
1 vegetable stock cube
500ml/18fl oz boiling water
400ml/14fl oz cider
2 tsp wholegrain mustard
8 Chantenay carrots, halved
    and ends removed
12 button mushrooms
Freshly ground black pepper

Heat the oven to 180°C/350°F/Gas mark 4.

Melt half of the butter in a large frying pan. Put the pork, bacon and onions into the pan and stir until they are all coated in the melted butter, then fry for 10 minutes on a medium heat, until the meat is browned and the onions are soft.

Add the dried sage and flour to the pan. Stir for a couple of minutes, over the heat, until the flour has disappeared.

Mix the vegetable stock cube with the boiling water and stir until it has dissolved. Add the cider to the stock, then slowly add the cider stock to the pan, a little at a time, stirring continuously to remove any lumps. The sauce should begin to thicken. When all of the stock is used up, stir in the mustard and transfer the contents of the pan to a casserole dish.

Put the remaining butter into the pan and stir on a low heat until it melts. Add the halved carrots and the button mushrooms and fry for 5 minutes, until they have a little colour. Put the mushrooms aside and add the carrots to the casserole. Season with pepper only; the bacon adds enough salt to this dish. Cover the casserole and cook in the oven for 45 minutes.

Remove from the oven, stir and return to the oven, uncovered, for a further 35 minutes. Add the mushrooms and cook for a further 10 minutes, uncovered. Remove and allow it to rest for a few minutes before serving.

7

SWEET TREATS

A dessert is a wonderful way to finish a great meal. They don't need to take hours to make; the recipes in this chapter are proof of that. Simple and delicious, they mostly have a hands-on time of less than 30 minutes and use ingredients that won't break the bank.

BLACK FOREST FROZEN YOGHURT

This is basically a cheat's ice-cream. It doesn't require an ice-cream maker or regular churning and it can be made ahead of time. This is a grown-up pudding for lovers of the Black Forest Gateau and has all the flavours of the retro classic that inspired it!

MAKES 6–8 SLICES

500g/1lb 2oz frozen
    mixed berries with
    cherries, defrosted
100g/4oz icing sugar
300ml/10fl oz double cream
100g/4oz dark chocolate
2 tbsp Greek yoghurt

Line a 450g/1lb loaf tin with cling film, leaving some excess hanging over the sides to cover the top later.

Put the defrosted fruit into a saucepan with half the icing sugar. Simmer on a medium–high heat for 5 minutes, until the sugar has melted and the sauce has thickened a little. Set aside until completely cool.

Set a heatproof bowl above a pan of simmering water, making sure the base of the bowl is not touching the water. Break the chocolate into the bowl and melt over a low heat, stirring. Take off the heat once melted.

Pour the double cream into a mixing bowl and whisk it to stiff peaks with a hand-held electric whisk. Mix the remaining icing sugar into the cream along with the Greek yoghurt.

When the fruit is completely cool, use a potato masher to roughly crush the larger pieces of fruit, then pour this into the cream and fold in until combined.

Pour the melted chocolate into the cream and gently swirl it around to create ripples. Pour the mixture into the lined tin, then gently fold the excess cling film over the top so that it is completely covered. Put in the freezer for 5 hours, or overnight.

Remove the tin from the freezer and place in the fridge 30 minutes before serving. To turn it out, tip it upside down onto a chopping board, remove the cling film and cut into slices. Do not refreeze.

BLUEBERRY CRUNCH

This is definitely a cheat's pudding! It is not so much a recipe as an arrangement of food. It is, however, too good to leave out of the book. Granola is fantastic in a dessert – it's so sweet and crunchy. You can use any flavour you like. This is a birthday breakfast in our house, but you can have it anytime.

 FEEDS 2

150g/5oz blueberries
4 tbsp Greek yoghurt
2 large handfuls of granola
Drizzle of honey

Divide the blueberries between 2 bowls and put 2 tablespoons of yoghurt over each. Top each bowl with a large handful of granola and drizzle with a little honey.

PEANUT BUTTER SEED BALLS

These are lots of fun to make and the finished article is actually pretty healthy! These seed balls are packed full of protein and make a great mid-afternoon pick-me-up. They are so simple to make, they don't even require baking. Making these will get your hands satisfyingly messy, while only using one bowl!

 MAKES 12   ❄ **FREEZABLE**

70g/3oz seed mix
100g/4oz porridge oats
100g/4oz finely
    chopped prunes
100g/4oz finely chopped
    dark chocolate (optional)
5 tbsp peanut butter
2 tbsp honey

Add the seed mix, porridge oats, chopped prunes and chocolate, if using, to a mixing bowl and combine. Using your hands, mix the peanut butter and honey into the dry ingredients, firmly pressing everything together. This will take a couple of minutes.

When it is a consistent dough texture, divide the mixture into 12 and press each lump together firmly. Roll them into equal-sized balls in the palms of your hands. You can eat these immediately, or cover in cling film and store in the fridge for up to one week.

MINT AND PISTACHIO CHOCOLATE POTS

The great thing about this dessert is that it takes just 10 minutes to make. This can be made ahead of time and then whipped out of the fridge 10 minutes before eating. You can make this without the mint if you're not a fan, but the pistachio nuts give it a lovely crunch, so do include these if you can.

 MAKES 4 POTS

100g/4oz milk chocolate
300ml/10fl oz double cream
1 peppermint tea bag
2 tsp very finely chopped
    mint leaves (you can use
    a pestle and mortar)
Handful of shelled and
    crushed pistachio nuts

Set a heatproof bowl above a pan of simmering water, making sure that the base of the bowl is not touching the water. Break the chocolate into the bowl and melt it over a low heat, stirring.

Pour the cream into a separate mixing bowl. Dip the peppermint tea bag briefly in some boiling water and then put the tea bag into the cream. Leave it to soak for 5 minutes.

Remove the tea bag, giving it a little squeeze to get the flavour into the cream, then whip the cream until it starts to thicken. Fold in the melted chocolate and mint leaves and when the mixture is smooth and a single colour, divide it between 4 ramekins or serving glasses. Put the chocolate pots in the fridge for 2 hours, or overnight if you're making ahead.

Sprinkle with the crushed pistachio nuts before serving.

15-MINUTE APPLE AND BLACKBERRY CRUMBLES

Crumble is one of my favourite desserts. Seasonal fruit with a sweet crispy topping reminds me of autumn. The only problem with this pudding is that it traditionally takes such a long time to bake in the oven. So I've created this speedy recipe, so that when you get home from blackberry picking (or the supermarket!), with your containers brimming over with delicious fruit, you can knock up a crumble in a matter of minutes!

 MAKES 4

❄️ **FREEZABLE**

200g/7oz blackberries
2 eating apples, peeled, cored
    and cut into small chunks
2 tbsp water
3 tsp sugar
Double cream, to serve

FOR THE CRUMBLE TOPPING
75g/3oz plain flour
45g/2oz sugar
1 tsp ground cinnamon
20g/¾oz almond flakes
30g/1oz butter

Add the blackberries, apples, water and sugar to a large saucepan. Bring to the boil and simmer for 5 minutes until the apple is tender, stirring regularly. Divide the cooked fruit between 4 ramekins and allow to cool a little.

Meanwhile, make the crumble topping. Put the flour, sugar and cinnamon into a mixing bowl. Using your hands or a rolling pin, gently crush the almond flakes before adding them to the bowl. Work the butter through the dry ingredients with the tips of your fingers, until it resembles breadcrumbs. Add the crumble mix to a dry, non-stick frying pan and on a medium heat, toast it for 5 minutes, shaking the pan regularly so that it doesn't burn.

Divide the crumble topping among the ramekins, covering the fruit. Allow them to sit for a couple of minutes, so that the topping becomes crisp.

Serve with a dollop of cream.

LEMON AND GINGER CAKE

You will notice from the ingredients that I use the contents of a lemon and ginger tea bag – it actually works brilliantly! It gives a little crunch and sharpness to the sugary icing and goes well with the milder flavours of the sponge. (I use the same brand of tea bag each time but do check that yours is safe to eat!)

MAKES 10–12 SLICES

FREEZABLE

FOR THE SPONGE

200g/7oz self-raising flour
200g/7oz caster sugar
200g/7oz butter, softened
4 eggs, beaten
1 tsp baking powder
2 tsp ground ginger
Finely grated zest and
    juice of 2 lemons, plus
    extra to decorate

FOR THE ICING

1 lemon and ginger tea bag
125g/4½oz icing sugar
80g/3oz butter, softened
125g/4½oz soft cheese
½ tsp ground ginger

Heat the oven to 180°C/350°F/Gas mark 4. Grease a 900g/2lb loaf tin.

Put all of the sponge ingredients into a large mixing bowl, including the ground ginger and lemon zest and juice. Beat with a wooden spoon until you have a smooth cake batter. (This is known as the all-in-one sponge method.) Pour the cake mix into the loaf tin and bake on the middle shelf of the oven for 50 minutes.

Meanwhile, put the lemon and ginger tea bag into a mug, cover in boiling water and leave to soak for 5 minutes.

Put the icing sugar and softened butter into a bowl and mix with a hand-held electric whisk. Add the soft cheese and beat with a wooden spoon, until thick and creamy. Squeeze the excess water from the tea bag, open it up and add the contents to the icing with the ground ginger. Mix well.

Take the cake out of the oven and leave to rest in the tin for 10 minutes. Turn the cake out onto a wire rack and allow it to cool down completely.

Spread the soft cheese icing thickly over the top of the cold sponge and serve with a little extra lemon zest scattered over.

FLAPJACK CAKES

I used to make these every week for my children after swimming. They are packed with fruit and have no added sugar – they get all their sweetness from the honey and fruit, so it's actually a pretty healthy snack. They are much more light and cakey than an ordinary flapjack.

MAKES 12 FLAPJACKS

FREEZABLE

100g/4oz butter, plus
    extra for greasing
4 tbsp honey
1 tsp ground cinnamon
200g/7oz porridge oats
100g/4oz self-raising flour
150g/5oz dried fruit (I use
    a combination of raisins
    and chopped prunes)
3 apples, peeled and grated

Heat the oven to 200°C/400°F/Gas mark 6. Grease a 30 × 20cm/12 × 8in baking tin with butter.

Put the butter and honey into a saucepan and melt on a low heat. Put all of the remaining ingredients into a mixing bowl and pour the melted butter and honey over the top. Mix thoroughly.

Pour the mixture into the baking tin, pressing it down gently. Bake for 15–20 minutes, until it is starting to turn golden brown. Leave to cool in the tin.

Once cool, cut into slices or squares and serve.

EARL GREY MALT LOAF

This is my version of the traditional malt loaf. It has a wonderfully dense and sticky texture, and is perfect served warm, with plenty of butter. The bran flakes give it a deep malty flavour and I use golden syrup instead of treacle to make it lighter. You can use ordinary tea rather than Earl Grey, but I think this type of tea really does add something extra to the flavour.

MAKES 1 LOAF

FREEZABLE

100g/4oz bran flakes
Mug of Earl Grey tea
200g/7oz self-raising flour
200g/7oz light brown sugar
1 tbsp golden syrup
180g/6oz sultanas
1 tsp baking powder
1 egg, beaten

Soak the bran flakes in a bowl with the tea for 30 minutes.

Heat the oven to 180°C/350°F/Gas mark 4. Grease or line a 900g/2lb loaf tin.

In a large mixing bowl, combine the flour, sugar, golden syrup, sultanas, baking powder and beaten egg. Stir with a wooden spoon, working in the soaked bran flakes, too. Don't worry if there is some excess tea, this can go in as well.

Pour the cake mixture into the tin and bake in the oven for 1 hour. Leave to cool in the tin for 10 minutes, before turning out onto a wire rack.

Serve warm, cut into slices, with butter.

CHOCOLATE BRIOCHE PUDDING

You can't beat a bread and butter pudding! This one uses chocolate-chip brioche buns instead of bread, so you get a lovely melted chocolate taste in with the pudding. You can substitute the cream for all milk if you prefer.

FEEDS 4

❄ **FREEZABLE**

25g/1oz butter, plus
    extra for greasing
8 chocolate chip brioche rolls
50g/2oz raisins
400ml/14fl oz milk
50ml/2fl oz double cream
1 tsp ground cinnamon
3 eggs
75g/3oz caster sugar

Heat the oven to 190°C/375°F/Gas mark 5. Grease a deep ovenproof dish about 25 × 20 × 7cm/10 × 8 × 2¾.

Cut each of the brioche rolls in half lengthways and then in half again widthways.

Butter the insides of the rolls and place them, slightly overlapping, in the baking dish – there should be at least two layers. Sprinkle the raisins between the layers as you go.

Pour the milk and cream into a saucepan and stir in the cinnamon. On a medium heat, warm the milk through without bringing it to the boil.

In a mixing bowl, whisk the eggs and sugar together until they are pale in colour. When the milk is hot, pour it onto the eggs and sugar, stirring well.

Pour this mixture over the brioche in the dish and bake in the oven for 45 minutes, until golden and bubbling.

BANANA AND CHOCOLATE MUFFINS

I went through a stage a couple of years ago when I made muffins all the time. Muffins aren't like a sponge: a sponge has a basic recipe, which only varies slightly. Muffin recipes, on the other hand, can use entirely different ingredients, depending on where you look. I have had many muffin failures, so I wanted to include a really good recipe that will give you both rise and moistness every time!

MAKES 8 LARGE MUFFINS

FREEZABLE

3 very ripe bananas
50ml/2fl oz light olive oil
1 tbsp milk
150g/5oz milk chocolate
110g/4¼oz self-raising flour
100g/4oz brown sugar
1 tbsp cocoa powder
½ tsp baking powder

Heat the oven to 180°C/350°F/Gas mark 4. Line a muffin tin with 8 paper cases.

In a mixing bowl, mash the bananas with a fork. Add the oil and milk to the bananas and stir.

Set a heatproof bowl above a pan of simmering water, making sure that the base of the bowl is not touching the water. Break half the chocolate into the bowl and melt it over a low heat, stirring. Take off the heat once melted and add to the banana mixture.

In a separate bowl, combine the flour, sugar, cocoa powder and baking powder. Chop the remaining chocolate into small chunks and add to the flour, making sure all of the ingredients are combined. Add the dry ingredients to the banana mixture and beat lightly.

Spoon the mixture into the paper cases and bake in the oven for 30 minutes.

MIXED BERRY AND WHITE CHOCOLATE COOKIES

You can put most things into a buttery biscuit mix and it will taste good, but this combination is a particularly good one. The sharpness of the berries stops the white chocolate making the biscuits too sweet. Change the flavour by making the basic biscuit recipe and adding anything you like.

MAKES 8 BISCUITS

FREEZABLE

125g/4½oz butter, softened, plus extra for greasing
70g/3oz sugar
1 egg, beaten
70g/3oz dried mixed berries
150g/5oz plain flour
100g/4oz white chocolate, chopped into small chunks

Cream the butter and sugar together in a large mixing bowl, then stir in the beaten egg.

In a separate bowl combine the dried berries and the flour, then mix in the chocolate. Tip this mixture into the creamed butter mixture and mix thoroughly until it forms a dough. Roll the dough into a ball, wrap it in cling film and put it in the fridge for 30 minutes.

Heat the oven to 180°C/350°F/Gas mark 4. Grease a large baking tray.

Roll the dough out to roughly 1–2cm/½–¾in thick and, using the top of a mug or a biscuit cutter, cut out 8 circles, approximately 8cm/3in in diameter.

Put the biscuits onto the baking tray and bake in the oven for 12–15 minutes, until lightly golden around the edges. Transfer to a wire rack to cool for at least 20 minutes.

about the AUTHOR

Amy Sheppard is a busy mum of two boys, living in Cornwall.
Amy grew up in Cornwall and was taught to cook by her Mum.
There was never very much money, so the key was cooking great
food on a budget, by shopping smart and using up leftovers.
When Amy became a stay-at-home mum, the reduction in
income meant that she had to be more frugal and imaginative in
the way that she shopped and cooked. Returning to the cooking
style she was brought up on, Amy began to develop simple
budget recipes for her own family.

This book was written with busy people in mind; enabling
them to get everything they need from discount supermarkets,
by providing simple, healthy meal ideas that don't cost
the earth.

INDEX

ACKNOWLEDGEMENTS

Thank you…

Apologies for the indulgence in acknowledging so many people! The completion of this book really has been a team effort and so I hope you'll forgive me for thanking everyone that has played a part.

Thank you to my endlessly patient husband Paul for your love, support and honesty! With love to my wonderful boys, Elliot and Sam – you two really are my greatest joy and I wouldn't have written this book without you.

My parents, who have supported me in everything I have ever done. My brilliant Mum for going through the book with a fine toothcomb, and for your daily encouragement and kindness.

To my lovely brother Charlie, for making me realise that this just might be possible!

Amy Cassidy for the beautiful family photos in this book and for your daily encouragement and friendship.

To Howard Shooter and Denise Smart for the beautiful food photography and styling.

Juliana Johnston, for my lovely publicity photos.

A huge thank you to the incredible team at Ebury and in particular Lydia Good for all of your hard work and for making this book more than I ever could have imagined.

Clare Hulton, my literary agent, for seeing the potential in this book and for your support and wise words!

To Therese Fozard, Soraya Fawcus, Amy Cronin, Duncan and Sarah Chown for your friendship and support.

Lastly, I would like to thank all of my followers on Instagram and Facebook for all of your kind words over the last year.

I feel incredibly lucky You have all helped turn my dream into a reality.

A x

1 3 5 7 9 10 8 6 4 2

Ebury Press, an imprint of Ebury Publishing,
20 Vauxhall Bridge Road,
London SW1V 2SA

Ebury Press is part of the Penguin Random House group
of companies whose addresses can be found at global.
penguinrandomhouse.com

Penguin
Random House
UK

Food photography: Howard Shooter
Food styling: Denise Smart
Design: Gemma Wilson
Editor: Lydia Good
Photography on p.68 Juliana Johnston
Photography on p.174 Amy Cassidy
Illustrations: Shutterstock

First published by Ebury Press in 2017

www.penguin.co.uk

A CIP catalogue record for this book is available from the British
Library

ISBN 9781785035968

Printed and bound in Italy by L.E.G.O. S.p.A